A Prayer for Baby

A Prayer for Baby
A 40-Week Pregnancy Daily Devotional

Rosalynn M. Smith, Ph.D

"And all thy children shall be taught of the Lord; and great shall be the peace of thy children" (Isaiah 54:13, KJV).

Copyright © 2015 Rosalynn M. Smith, Ph.D.

All rights reserved. No part of this book may be used or reproduced by any means, graphic, electronic, or mechanical, including photocopying, recording, taping or by any information storage retrieval system without the written permission of the author except in the case of brief quotations embodied in critical articles and reviews.

Cover Drawing by: Roger B. Manor
Author Photo Copyright: Amy Headington Images of Grace Photography

Scripture quotations taken from the Holy Bible, New Living Translation, copyright 1996, 2004. Used by permission of Tyndale House Publishers, Inc., Wheaton, Illinois 60189. All rights reserved.

Scripture quotations taken from the New American Standard Bible®, Copyright © 1960, 1962, 1963, 1968, 1971, 1972, 1973, 1975, 1977, 1995 by The Lockman Foundation. Used by permission." (www.Lockman.org)

Scripture taken from the Holy Bible, New International Version®. Copyright © 1973, 1978, 1984 Biblica. Used by permission of Zondervan. All rights reserved.

Scripture taken from the New King James Version. Copyright 1979, 1980, 1982 by Thomas Nelson, inc. Used by permission. All rights reserved.

Scripture is taken from GOD'S WORD®, © 1995 God's Word to the Nations. Used by permission of Baker Publishing Group.

WestBow Press books may be ordered through booksellers or by contacting:

WestBow Press
A Division of Thomas Nelson & Zondervan
1663 Liberty Drive
Bloomington, IN 47403
www.westbowpress.com
1 (866) 928-1240

Because of the dynamic nature of the Internet, any web addresses or links contained in this book may have changed since publication and may no longer be valid. The views expressed in this work are solely those of the author and do not necessarily reflect the views of the publisher, and the publisher hereby disclaims any responsibility for them.

Any people depicted in stock imagery provided by Thinkstock are models, and such images are being used for illustrative purposes only. Certain stock imagery © Thinkstock.

ISBN: 978-1-4908-9233-7 (sc)
ISBN: 978-1-4908-9235-1 (hc)
ISBN: 978-1-4908-9234-4 (e)

Print information available on the last page.

WestBow Press rev. date: 10/09/2015

*This book is dedicated to Bradley I and Bradley II (Alex).
God, thank You for answering my prayers.*

Introduction

Months before becoming pregnant, I began conducting scientific research at a local neonatal intensive care unit (NICU). Each week, as I listened to the doctors describe the conditions of the tiny patients, my heart would feel great compassion for the new baby, mommy, and family. As the doctors spewed out the statistical data that went along with each ailment, I assured myself that my unborn (and at the time, not yet conceived) child would not be a victim of medical statistics.

My answer to medical statistics was *prayer*. Therefore, I prayed daily for my child as my child grew within me. I prayed for every aspect of my baby's growth and development. God—and God alone—would have the final say in my baby's life. The voice of medical statistics is silenced here!

The prayers you will read in the coming days were birthed from experience—the ultimate research. During my forty-week pregnancy, I sought God daily. Knowing that God alone is the creator of life, my goal was simply to confess His Word and promises for my baby and my family. I provided God an open invitation to be in control of every aspect of my pregnancy and life. Giving God full reign in my pregnancy removed my fears and allowed me to have a peaceful pregnancy.

As you read each prayer, you are encouraged to review key Scriptures provided in the daily prayers. Allow the Scriptures and prayers to become part of your daily living. When possible, read aloud, sharing the promises of God with your new baby and growing family.

Each week, a journal—My Letter to Baby—is provided to keep your baby updated on the amazing adventures of your journey through pregnancy. Allow your letters to become a reminder to you and your baby of God's amazing grace for years to come!

Weeks 1–3

*"I waited patiently for the Lord; He turned to me
and heard my cry" (Psalm 40:1, NIV).*

God, thank You for being patient with me. You sent me this baby in Your perfect time. Like Rebekah, I did not know when this time would come; but like Isaac, I knew I served an unfailing God. From the millions of eggs You gave me at birth, You waited for the release of the perfect one. Thank You for perfecting the union of my husband's sperm and my egg—a scientific phenomenon that could only be arranged by You. As your master plan of conception unfolds in the coming weeks, prepare me to care for my baby as You have cared for me. "You gave me life and showed me your unfailing love. My life was preserved by your care" (Job 10:12, NLT). You have known this baby since the beginning of time (Isaiah 41:4); therefore, God, teach me Your ways so that I may raise my baby according to Your perfect plan for my baby's life. God, You know the plans You have for my baby: plans of good and not of disaster, plans to give my baby a future and a hope (Jeremiah 29:11). Please, give this baby a wonderful future and enduring hope. In Jesus' name. Amen.

My Letter to Baby: Date: _____

Week 4

"May the God of your father help you; May the Almighty bless you with the blessings of the heavens above ... and blessings of the breasts and womb" (Genesis 49:25, NLT).

Day 1

God, thank You for another day to be in your presence and bask in Your glory. We recognize You as the God that has made us and gives us life (Job 33:4). This week, you have assigned the organs to begin to form in baby. Baby's embryo, formed of the epiblast and the hypoblast, are preparing a place for the organs to grow. Take special care to protect and perfect the growth of baby's organs. You have created spaces in my womb for my blood to flow to the developing placenta. Purify my blood of diseases and dangers—seen and unseen—so that baby receives proper nutrients and oxygen during development. As You meticulously form baby in my womb, please allow baby to daily feel Your presence (1 Chronicles 16:27), peace (John 14:27), and Your Holy Spirit (John 14:16). Correct my diet and my exercise to accommodate the new life You have entrusted to me. We love You, God, and bless Your holy name—this day and always. In Jesus' name. Amen.

Day 2

God, thank You for being our God. "Now our Lord Jesus Christ himself, and God, even our Father, which hath loved us, and hath given us everlasting consolation and good hope through grace, comfort your hearts, and establish you in every good word and work" (2 Thessalonians 2:16, KJV). The news of our new baby feels amazing, and the thought of having a new life to care for is overwhelming at times. Please be our help. You have set in motion a phenomenon that cannot be duplicated or controlled by man. Therefore, we ask that You manage each step of baby's growth and development. As the amniotic sac (which houses baby) fills with amniotic fluid (to cushion baby), protect the amniotic fluid from bacteria or any infection that may try to invade the amniotic sac. We recognize that the fetal cells, chemicals, and microorganisms within the amniotic fluid provide an abundance of information regarding our baby's genetic makeup, present condition, and level of maturity. We thank you that the amniotic sac and amniotic fluid are safe from all harm. We rebuke any chromosomal abnormalities, metabolic disorders, or enzyme deficiencies of the amniotic fluid in Jesus' name. We thank You that any paternal and maternal genetic disorders (dominant and recessive) that could pass on to the fetus through the amniotic fluid (and otherwise) cease and desist right now. Neither disease nor fetal infection can dwell in or around our baby, because the blood of Jesus covers baby and destroys every yoke of bondage (including—but not limited to—sickness and disease). Please, God, perfect baby's growth within the amniotic sac and keep baby safe and comfortable. And if, by chance, amniocentesis is ever required, I thank You now for non-alarming and joy-filled results. As the red blood cells are produced by the yolk sac, we command the red blood cells to proliferate, propagate, and maintain the proper levels as originally intended by God—now and for all the days of baby's life. We command the yolk sac to properly deliver nutrients to baby until the placenta has fully developed. In Jesus' name. Amen.

Day 3

God, thank You for another day to acknowledge You as a wonderful God! "O Lord, you are my God; I will exalt you and praise your name, for in perfect faithfulness you have done marvelous things, things planned long ago" (Isaiah 25:1, NIV). We understand that although it is early, this week is a critical week in baby's gestation journey. Today, we pray for the top layer of the embryo—the ectoderm. As the ectoderm gives rise to baby's central and peripheral nervous system, please perfect each aspect of the nervous system's development. Cast away any dysfunction that may attempt to disrupt the formation and activity of the nervous system—now and forevermore—in Jesus' name. You have set in motion the formation of the brain (forebrain, middle brain, and hindbrain), spinal cord, hair, and skin. Please perfect each of these areas; let baby be formed in your image (Genesis 1:26). As the eyes, inner ear, and connective tissues develop from the ectoderm, perfect baby's eyesight, hearing, senses, and sensations, for we know that You will perfect that which concerns us (Psalm 138:8). We love You, Jesus. Although we do not know every element that has to form and develop, we do know that You specialize in life (Genesis 1:27). Please take special care of the life and development of our baby. In Jesus' name. Amen.

Day 4

God, thank You for another day to marvel at your creation and to bless Your name. "We give thanks to you, O God, we give thanks, for your name is near; men tell of your wonderful deeds" (Psalm 75:1, NIV). We cannot feel everything that is occurring right now, but we know that You have set in motion the formation of baby's heart and primitive circulatory system. We ask that You carefully monitor the formation of the mesoderm, for this will be baby's life support system for his or her lifetime. The mesoderm, or middle layer of the embryo, will soon form baby's heart, sex organs, bones, kidneys, and muscles. I pray that our baby has a healthy heart, both physically and spiritually. Condition baby's heart—even in the womb—to be a heart like David's, created without the complications of life that David had to experience. Let my baby's heart always be true to You, God (1 Kings 8:61). Thank You that baby's reproductive system forms perfectly and that he or she is never confused about his or her sexuality. We proclaim that baby's bones and muscles are strong. I pray that baby is smart and athletic and that baby's body supports his or her will and determination. Please perfect the development of organs. Specifically, today I ask that you would perfect baby's kidneys as they form from the mesoderm. Please satisfy baby with long life and show baby your salvation (Psalm 91:16). In Jesus' name. Amen.

Day 5

God, thank You for revealing Your glory in our lives. Your glorious works are amazing (Psalm 77: 14). I cannot feel the movement of baby right now, nor can I see any major changes in my body; but I know You are working a marvelous miracle within me. Today, I pray for baby's lungs, intestines, and bladder as they form from the endoderm. I thank You that baby never suffers from any form of lung disease. As baby grows older, I thank You that he or she never has the desire to smoke or use a substance that will harm the lungs or body. I claim perfection in the formation, development, and working of the lungs. Thank You that baby's breath and lung activity perfectly commences upon birth. We rebuke asthma, chronic lung disease, or any sickness that may be linked to or caused by improper lung activity. Thank You that baby's intestines and bladder develop without consequence and that these organs always work properly. We thank You that no harm shall come nigh baby's dwelling (inside and outside the womb), because You have given

Your angels charge over baby (Psalm 91). I pray that You would instruct us on which obstetrician(s) to choose. I know You have already chosen the obstetrician and nurses to deliver baby. Please give the obstetrician and nurses wisdom, knowledge, and focus on what to do and how to do it. Allow me to ask the proper questions and take the proper precautions for the care and safety of my baby. Direct our every footstep (Psalm 85:13). In Jesus' name. Amen.

Day 6

God, thank You for this day and the blessings you have bestowed upon us. We asked life of thee, and You gave it to us (Psalm 21:4). Our baby is now the size of an apple seed and still has a long gestational journey ahead. However, You called this generation at the beginning of time (Isaiah 41:4). This baby has been in Your thoughts since the beginning of time. Although new to me, my baby is no stranger to You. Thank You for continuing to bless baby's growth. As we near the end of week four, the beginning of baby's mouth and tongue are discernible. As You perfect the formation of baby's mouth, lips, and tongue, please be in control of the words of baby's mouth (Psalm 141:3); keep baby's tongue from evil and baby's lips from speaking lies (Psalm 34:13). Additionally, direct the proper formation of baby's thyroid and lymphatic system. As the lung buds and heart continue to be established, perfect the present and future circulation and coordination of the heart and lungs. Baby's first, thin layer of skin is beginning to form. Thank You that baby's skin is made perfect. I pray that baby never suffers from any skin disease, rash, hives, or skin allergies or reactions. We rebuke any generational skin disorder, including (but not limited to) eczema and angioedema. Even as the legs and arms begin to form and develop this week, please perfect their growth and development. We rebuke hereditary and nonhereditary arm and leg issues. Thank You, even now, for setting perfection in motion for baby's walking, running, speed, agility, and mobile abilities. Perfect the growth, strength, and activity of baby's skeletal structure. In Jesus' name. Amen.

Day 7

God, thank You for baby. I have already fallen deeply in love with this wonderful gift You have brought to my life. Please prepare my heart and my soul to always love You first. Instruct me of how to teach my baby to love You above all else (Deuteronomy 6:5). Baby's growth is causing my body to change. Please help me to adapt to the changes I see and do not see. Prepare me to provide proper nutrition and exercise to my body for my baby. Help me to obtain proper rest and relaxation during my pregnancy and after baby is born. Bless my teeth and gums to sustain the changes that my body will see in the coming weeks. We rebuke tooth decay, gum disease, and any oral health issues that will cause bacteria to invade the placenta or that will cause me discomfort. If any dental work has to be done on my teeth or gums, please bless the work to be safe for baby and me in every aspect. If You will, God, as we near the time during which morning or day sickness initiates, ease the discomfort, pain, and sickness that I am scheduled to encounter. But, if this affliction must occur, help me to recognize that our light affliction, which is but for a moment, worketh for us a far more exceeding and eternal weight of glory (2 Corinthians 4:17). I also pray that You would bless my husband and my marriage. As we increase our family, increase the love we have for You and for one another. Help us to be kind to one another and tenderhearted, forgiving one another, even as God, for Christ's sake, hath forgiven us (Ephesians 4:32). Prepare _____, my husband, to love and care for our baby, for You have chosen my husband so that he will direct his children and his household to keep the way of the Lord by doing what is right and just, so that the Lord will bring about for _____(husband's name)_____ what He promised _____(husband's name)_____ (Genesis 18:19).

Increase our finances to support our family. We know that You shall supply all our needs according to Your riches in glory by Christ Jesus (Philippians 4:19). Where there is any fear within my husband or myself, cast the fear away and replace the fear with love, because there is no fear in love; but perfect love casteth out fear (1 John 4:18). We love You, God. Thank You for loving us. In Jesus' name. Amen.

My Letter to Baby: Date: _____

Week 5

"For You formed my inward parts; You covered me in my mother's womb" (Psalm 139:13, NKJV).

Day 1

God, thank You for Your awesome works in our lives and for the awesome works You are doing in baby's life even now (Psalm 111:2). We know that this week is a very important week in our baby's life. The progress and development of the organs, including the heart, during this week are significant to baby's life. Additionally, it is written that "as water reflects a face, so a man's heart reflects the man" (Proverbs 27:19, NIV). As You perfectly form baby's heart this week, please give baby a pure, loving, and kind heart—a heart that trusts and believes You. Let the rhythm of baby's heartbeat be controlled and the flow and pumping of blood be properly maintained, as You have intended. I pray that every chamber, ventricle, artery, valve, muscle, atrium, aorta, ductus arteriosus—every part of the heart, named and unnamed—be made perfect in size, shape, and function. Thank You that baby never experiences heart disease, heart failure, a heart murmur(s), or any heart malfunction. Guard baby's heart, for the heart shall determine the course of baby's life (Proverbs 4:23). In Jesus' name. Amen.

Day 2

God, thank You for being strong and mighty in our lives. "Who is this King of glory? The LORD strong and mighty, the LORD mighty in battle" (Psalm 24:8, NIV). You are a great savior, and You are worthy of all praise an admiration. As we come to You today, we pray for the creation and growth of baby's umbilical cord. You are the source of our baby's life, and You have created the umbilical cord to be a special link from me to my baby, which provides valuable resources to assist in the growth and maturation of baby while in my womb. As the umbilical cord develops, perfect the formation of the substance of the umbilical cord. Provide the proper number of arteries and veins to run through the umbilical cord, direct the arteries and veins to carry the nutrients and oxygen, dispose of waste appropriately, and properly carry out all functions originally commanded by God. Bless the growth and maturation of the stem cells provided within the umbilical cord. We command the stem cells to be healthy and work according to God's plan for them. Please allow the proper nutrient- and oxygen-rich blood to be correctly exchanged between the embryo and placenta. We rebuke any dysfunctions in the operations, position, or location of the umbilical cord. There will be no umbilical cord abnormalities. Thank You that during labor and delivery, the umbilical cord will stay properly positioned in every stage of labor. Additionally, thank You that the umbilical cord will be properly clamped after birth in a timely manner. Grant me and my family the understanding and knowledge to properly care for the umbilical cord stump after the birth of baby. Please watch over baby while he or she is being formed in my womb. Perfect everything that affects the baby inside and outside of my body and baby's body. "You watched me as I was being formed in utter seclusion, as I was woven together in the dark of the womb" (Psalm 139:15, NLT). In Jesus' name. Amen.

Week 5

Day 3

God, You are amazing in all Your ways. "His miraculous signs are impressive. He uses his power to do amazing things. His kingdom is an eternal kingdom. His power lasts from one generation to the next" (Daniel 4:3, GW). We honor You, and we will be careful to praise Your name forevermore. We stand in amazement at the intricacy of the body. You have formed the heart to provide oxygen- and nutrient-rich blood to the entire body. As baby's blood begins to pump this week, please bless each beat of baby's heart. Thank You that my baby never experiences blood pressure that is too low or high. With each beat of baby's heart, provide the proper amount of blood (with the necessary amount of oxygen) to the lungs and body. I pray that the Spirit of God dwells within baby's bloodstream, always protecting baby from blood-borne illness, infection, and disease. Thank You that baby's blood always delivers the proper amount of nutrients and oxygen to baby's cells and properly carries waste away from baby's cells. Please bless each part of baby's circulatory system: the coronary (heart) circulation, pulmonary (lungs) circulation, and systemic (blood vessels) circulation. I thank You that my baby will learn at an early age that although You purify and perfect his or her blood, this blood cannot save him or her; it is in You that we have redemption through YOUR blood—forgiveness of sins, in accordance with the riches of God's grace (Ephesians 1:7). In Jesus' name. Amen.

Day 4

God, thank You for the hedge of protection that You continuously place around us. "Every word of God proves true. He is a shield to all who come to him for protection" (Proverbs 30:5, NLT). Thank You for blessing baby as he or she continues to grow. I pray that You would remove any fear of miscarrying, for Your Word says "[t]here will be no miscarriages or infertility among your people, and I will give you long, full lives" (Exodus 23:26, NLT). I believe this Word for myself, every mother who is pregnant, and every woman who longs to give birth to a baby. Please honor Your Word on our behalf. We will forever worship You and give You all glory and honor. I pray that as baby continues to grow, You would bless each stage of development of the neural tube. We rebuke any type of neural tube deformity or inconsistency. You have created the neural tube to be the origin of the spinal cord and brain. Thank You for full and perfect development of the brain, spinal cord, backbone, and all associated nerves. Please bless and regulate my folic acid levels so that the folic acid levels would be as You require them to be. Supplement any needed folic acid with Your spiritual folic acid. We are thankful that in Your Word, You promised to perfect that which concerned us (Psalm 138:8). We receive Your promise. Please, forsake not the works of Your own hands (Psalm 138:8). In Jesus' name. Amen.

Day 5

God, thank You for this day You have so graciously blessed us with. We love You and are thankful for the opportunity to praise Your righteous name. "Praise the LORD. Praise God in his sanctuary; praise him in his mighty heavens" (Psalm 150:1, NIV). I pray that today, as my baby's organs continue to develop, You would let Your hand guide and perfect the growth and placement of baby's organs. Please position each organ to be in its perfect place. Bless the life and health of each organ, and allow baby's organs and tissues to receive proper nourishment. Thank You that each organ functions according to the organ's specialized purpose. As baby's arms and legs grow and develop, please allow the arms and legs to develop in perfection. Bless each limb, finger, and toe to grow to the appropriate length and strength, for "the arms of his hands were made strong by the hands of the mighty God of Jacob" (Genesis 49:24, KJV). Allow the arms, fingers, legs, and toes to operate properly all the days of baby's life. As You gave Elijah strength and speed to run ahead of Ahab's chariot (1 Kings 18:46), please give baby strength and phenomenal speed. If it be Your will, bless baby to be a great athlete with strong bones and muscles. Thank You for blessing the maturation of baby in my womb. We praise You that our baby is fearfully and wonderfully made. "I will praise thee; for I am fearfully *and* wonderfully made: marvellous *are* thy works; and *that* my soul knoweth right well" (Psalm 139:14, KJV). In Jesus' name. Amen.

Day 6

God, thank You for the blessings You have bestowed upon us. "Even by the God of thy father, who shall help thee; and by the Almighty, who shall bless thee with blessings of heaven above, blessings of the deep that lieth under, blessings of the breasts, and of the womb" (Genesis 49:25, KJV). We praise You for what You have done in our lives and all that You are willing to do. We thank You that You alone are God, and of You, there is none other. Thank You for continuing to bless baby in my womb. As baby's brain continues to develop, please bless and perfect every aspect of baby's brain formation. Thank You that baby's brain and head are shaped properly (and are proportionally sized). I thank You that baby never suffers from any brain dysfunction. We rebuke stroke, headaches, and any dysfunction that may be caused by or is associated with the brain and brain activity. I thank You that every neuron in baby's brain processes and transmits information properly and efficiently. We pray that baby is a fast learner and is able to quickly and properly process information. Thank You that baby is smart, intelligent, and polite. I thank You that baby has a wonderful, fun personality and respects others—specifically, his or her parents—for Your Word says, "[c]hildren, obey your parents in everything, for this pleases the Lord" (Colossians 3:20, NIV). We live our lives to please You, Lord (2 Corinthians 5:9). In Jesus' name. Amen.

Day 7

God, thank You for bringing us through baby's fifth week of life. "In him was life" (John 1:4, NIV). As we embark on another week of baby's life, development, and growth, give us direction of what type of parents to be. I pray that You would give us knowledge of how to raise baby in the church and how to teach baby Your way. Surround our baby with positive family members and friends. Bless baby's church family to be strong, loving, caring, and a great example for baby. Help my husband and me to be wonderful parents and role models for our baby. As our baby begins to have an influence on others, bless him or her to exude Your love and be a Christian example to others. Help me to teach our baby the Bible, Bible verses, the books of the Bible, and the attributes the Bible says we are to encompass. Let our home be a house of love, joy, and peace. Please let Your Spirit rest, rule, and abide in our lives henceforth and forevermore. In Jesus' name. Amen.

My Letter to Baby: Date: _____

Week 6

"Before I formed thee in the belly I knew thee; and before thou camest forth out of the womb I sanctified thee, [and] I ordained thee a prophet unto the nations" (Jeremiah 1:5, KJV).

Day 1

God, thank You for keeping Your promises. "And being fully persuaded that, what he had promised, he was able also to perform" (Romans 4:21, KJV). You are an amazing God, and it is a privilege to praise You. I grow more and more anxious by the day—anxious for the next doctor's appointment, anxious to share the news of baby, anxious to see our baby, anxious to see what the next months of my life will bring. But Your Word says, "be anxious for nothing, but in everything by prayer and supplication with thanksgiving let your requests be made known to God" (Philippians 4:6). Please help us to trust You and to trust Your timing. Remove the anxiety, and let us be careful to seek You daily in all things. Please continue to bless baby's development. As baby's arms and legs continue to develop, bless each bone, muscle, nerve, and ligament to properly form and grow. Thank You that baby's two complete arms and legs are perfectly made and perfectly functional. Thank You that baby's fingers and toes are anointed of God. Your Word says You have given baby every place that the soles of his or her feet shall tread upon (Joshua 1:3). Please bless my baby to take dominion over every ground he or she treads upon and over the works of Your hands, for You have put all things under his or her feet (Psalm 8:6). Please bless baby with special gifts to worship You with his or her hands. Specifically, we pray for baby to be musically inclined to play the piano or an instrument that pleases you. Thank You, Lord! In Jesus' name. Amen.

Day 2

God, thank You that we can come to You at any time of the day and that You hear us. "Save, LORD: let the King hear us when we call" (Psalm 20:9, KJV). Today we give You permission to guide our emotions, and we thank You for peace that surpasses all understanding (Isaiah 26:3). Throughout our pregnancy—and even after baby's birth—baby's brain will continue to grow and develop. Please bless each phase of growth and development of baby's brain. I thank You that baby produces all the neurons You have designed him or her to produce. Thank You for perfecting baby's pituitary gland as it begins to form this week, as it will secrete hormones that are essential to baby's growth and reproduction. Please watch over and sanctify every part of baby's brain development. Bless baby's skull to securely hold and protect the brain You have preciously created. Thank You that no sickness or disease shall ever plague baby's brain. Father, as You gave wisdom, knowledge, riches, wealth, and honor unto Solomon, please give wisdom, knowledge, riches, wealth, and honor unto my baby. "Wisdom and knowledge is granted unto thee; and I will give thee riches, and wealth, and honour" (2 Chronicles 1:23, KJV). In Jesus' name. Amen.

Day 3

God, thank You for declaring war on our enemies and for protecting us, Your children. You will keep us from all harm. You watch over our lives (Psalm 121:7). As baby's eyes and eye lenses begin to form and develop, please perfect baby's vision. Thank You that baby's physical vision is better than man's definition of perfect. We recognize that You have created the eyes and eyesight to be extremely complex. Man could never recreate all the optics, physics, light waves, chemical reactions, and electrical impulses that work together with split-second precision to formulate the images our eyes present to our brains; but You, Lord, are the master engineer. We cannot name every component and feature that works to create sight; so we pray that You would perfect that which You have created. Please perfect baby's eyes and eyesight. Even more importantly, sanctify baby's spiritual vision. Let Your Holy Spirit give baby sight and allow him or her to see what You would have him or her to see. Bless baby's spiritual vision to comprehend the spiritual realities of life, so that he or she may see the light of the glorious gospel of Christ, who is the image of God (2 Corinthians 4:4). In Jesus' name. Amen.

Day 4

God, thank You for blessing us exceedingly and abundantly above all that we ask or think according to the power that worketh in us (Ephesians 3:20). We cannot see the progress of baby's development, but we know that You have put into progression a glorious work. Please bless the baby's face and facial features as they develop. Thank You that baby's nose and nostrils are positioned properly and sized to perfection. Thank You for blessing baby's sense of smell, breathing, and all activity that You have created the nose to be responsible for. Perfect the hairs and mucus that protect the brain and body, and keep airborne diseases from entering baby's body. Bless each nerve that runs from the nose to the brain. Bless the position, size, and shape of baby's mouth and lips. Please, I pray that as baby grows, You would set a watch, O Lord, before my baby's mouth and keep the door of my baby's lips (Psalm 141:3). Bless the words of my mouth and the meditations of my heart to please You, for my baby will mimic my words and actions. Perfect the formation and functionality of baby's ears. Thank You that baby hears well and is obedient to his or her parents when he or she hears instructions; for if our baby honors his or her father and mother, then his or her days may be long upon the land which the Lord God gives (Exodus 20:12). I pray that baby has a beautiful countenance and is goodly to look to, as David ("Now he was ruddy, and withal of a beautiful countenance, and goodly to look to" [1 Samuel 16:12].) or Rachel ("but Rachel was beautiful and well favoured" [Genesis 29:17]). Thank you that baby is blessed and highly favored of the Lord. We bless You in advance that our baby never experiences a broken facial bone and that his or her face and features are made perfect in You. In Jesus' name. Amen.

Day 5

God, thank You that You are God alone. You never stop being a great God. Thank You. It is wonderful to think of baby forming in my womb; however, sometimes I worry about the days to come—pregnancy, birth, and child-rearing. But today, I turn my worry into worship—I will give unto the Lord the glory due unto his name; I worship the Lord in the beauty of holiness (Psalm 29:2). Please forgive me for worrying and help me to trust You all the more. Today, I pray that You would bless the formation and development of baby's intestines. Perfect the functionality, shape, length, size, position, and location of the intestines. Thank You that baby does not suffer from gastroschisis at birth. We bless You now that baby never suffers from any intestinal disease or dysfunction. Thank You that all parts of the small and large intestines work properly to digest baby's food—from infancy throughout the adult years. Please bless and perfect the inward parts of baby. In Jesus' name. Amen.

Day 6

God, thank You for Your faithfulness. "I do not hide your righteousness in my heart; I speak of your faithfulness and salvation" (Psalm 40:10, NIV). Thank You that no matter what things look like, You remain God, and You are always in control. Thank You for the growth and maturation of the baby inside of me. We cannot see the miraculous details You have set in motion at the molecular level, but we know that Your plans for baby's life, body, and abilities are in motion. As baby's pancreas grows and develops this week, we pray that You would cover, protect, and bless baby's pancreas. Thank You that baby's pancreas properly enables baby to handle digestive enzymes. We rebuke any dysfunction in enzyme production or processing. Thank You that baby's pancreas is properly equipped to process the insulin and glucagon that the body needs to function. Bless baby's pancreas to always produce the proper amount of insulin. Thank You that baby's pancreas always works properly and that baby never develops pancreatitis, pancreatic cancer, an injured pancreas, or any pancreatic dysfunction. God, You designed the pancreas to operate in a particular fashion. Please do not allow baby's pancreas or the organs associated with the activity of the pancreas to ever operate out of line with Your will. We thank You for blessing baby to maintain an appropriate diet. Regulate baby's mind to properly take care of the temple You have graciously given our baby. Please keep baby mindful that his or her body is the temple of God. "Know ye not that ye are the temple of God, and that the Spirit of God dwelleth in you? If any man defile the temple of God, him shall God destroy; for the temple of God is holy, which temple ye are" (1 Corinthians 3:16–17, KJV). In Jesus' name. Amen.

Day 7

God, thank You that we don't have to leave baby's life, body, and abilities to the chance of medical and social statistics, but that we can bring our cares and concerns directly to our heavenly Father. "Casting all your care upon him; for he careth for you" (1 Peter 5:7). We are thankful that You, Lord, are the ultimate decision-maker in our baby's life—most importantly, You care for our baby. I pray that baby and his or her daddy will have an incredible relationship for all the days of their lives. Thank You that baby's daddy loves and cares for him or her as you love and care for Your children. I thank You that regardless of my husband's previous maternal and paternal relationship(s), You will provide an unimaginable love between daddy and baby—a love that is new and unique to baby and daddy alone. I pray that my husband teaches baby to "hear the instruction of thy father, and forsake not the law of thy mother" (Proverbs 1:8, KJV). O God, please deposit in baby the desire to honor his or her father and mother so his or her days may be long upon the land which the Lord God gives (Exodus 20:12). In Jesus' name. Amen.

My Letter to Baby: Date: _____

Week 7

"For I was born a sinner—yes, from the moment my mother conceived me. But you desire honesty from the womb, teaching me wisdom even there" (Psalm 51:5–6, NLT).

Day 1

God, thank You for Your loving kindness and tender mercies. "Do not withhold your mercy from me, O LORD; may your love and your truth always protect me" (Psalm 40:11, NIV). We pray that as baby's hands and feet emerge from the developing arms and legs, You would not only perfect the development of baby's arms, legs, hands, and feet, but even as baby matures in my womb, perfect baby's praise. Thank You that we will teach baby as an infant to praise You in song, in dance, and with the clapping of hands (Psalms 47, 149). Thank You, God, for attending to every detail of baby's development. Thank You that each finger and toe forms perfectly. Please bless baby's elbows and knees as they learn to bend and move. Bless every muscle and nerve in baby's arms and legs. Thank You that baby's arms, legs, hands, and feet function with perfection. I thank You that baby never suffers from broken bones, joint problems, or muscle or ligament problems, nor arm, leg, hand, or foot dysfunction.

"He keepeth all his bones: not one of them is broke" (Psalm 34:20). In Jesus' name. Amen.

Day 2

God, thank You for sacrificing Your only son that we may have life and have life more abundantly (John 10:10). You have been a generous God, and we appreciate You. We pray that You would bless baby's eyes and eyelids as they form and mature. Thank You for perfecting baby's eyesight as well as the shape, color, and position of his or her eyes. I pray that every muscle, nerve, and vessel in baby's eyes function properly. Thank You that baby always has great vision—both physically and spiritually. Please bless baby's nose as it forms and develops on the face. I pray that the nose always functions properly and is perfectly shaped and positioned on baby's face. As baby's veins establish their position and purpose throughout his or her body, I pray that the veins are properly placed and perform their job with perfection. Lord, we know that Your eyes run to and fro throughout the whole earth to show Yourself strong on behalf of them whose hearts are perfect toward you (2 Chronicles 16:9). Our hearts love You. Please, show yourself strong on our behalf; bless our lives, and bless our baby. In Jesus' name. Amen.

Day 3

God, thank You for having *all* power of both heaven and earth in Your hands (Matthew 28:18). We find comfort in knowing that You are the giver of life and every good and perfect gift (James 1:17). We thank You that baby is a good and perfect gift that has come from our Father in heaven. We ask that as baby continues to grow and mature in my womb, You would continue to perfect the gift You have given to us. Please bless baby's brain development and maturation. As baby's brain hemispheres grow, I pray that the left and right brain hemispheres function to perfection. Among the many brain functions of the left hemisphere, please guide with precision the attributes that control baby's understanding and use of language (listening, reading, speaking, and writing), memory (for spoken and written messages), detailed analysis of information, and the functions of the right side of the body. Along with the left hemisphere activities, please structure the right hemisphere activities to correctly judge the position of things in space, know body position, understand and remember things done and seen, process information to form an entire picture, and control the left side of the body. Please bless all functions of each hemisphere of baby's brain—known and unknown, seen and unseen. Thank You that my baby never suffers from stroke, aneurism, or any form of brain injury. O, Lord, You are the God of my baby's health and strength, and I am confident of this very thing—that He who began a good work in my husband, me, and our baby will perfect it until the day of Christ Jesus (Philippians 1:6). In Jesus' name. Amen.

Day 4

God, thank You for Your perfect love. You are an amazing God, and You give me no reason to doubt You. I find no fault in You, Lord. Thank You for continuing to bless and anoint baby. I pray that as baby's liver develops and grows this week, You would please bless and sanctify the liver. Thank You that the liver will perform perfectly to accomplish the many functions You assigned to the liver when creating man, including (but not limited to) detoxification, protein synthesis, and production of biochemicals necessary for digestion. Thank You that baby never suffers from liver problems or liver failure. Additionally, as baby's red blood cells mature and proliferate, we pray that You would sanctify baby's red blood cells. Thank You that baby always has the proper number of healthy red blood cells.

We command the red blood cells to effectively and efficiently carry out all duties assigned by God, including delivering oxygen to the tissues and bonding with the tissue's carbon dioxide or other waste gases to transport the carbon dioxide and waste gases away. Thank You, Lord, for so graciously creating man in Your image (Genesis 1:27). Thank You that our baby is made perfect in You. "Be ye therefore perfect, even as your Father which is in heaven is perfect" (Matthew 5:48, KJV). In Jesus' name. Amen.

Day 5

God, thank You that heaven is Your throne, and the earth is Your footstool (Isaiah 66:1); therefore, we sit at Your feet on earth and worship You. We have come to adore You today, because You alone are worthy! Thank You for the continued progression of baby's appendix and pancreas. Although the function of the appendix is not completely clear to modern scientists and doctors, You made the appendix and have placed the appendix within our bodies for a particular reason. I pray that You take care of baby's appendix. Thank You that the appendix is properly placed within baby's body and functions according to Your will. Thank You that as baby grows, he or she never develops appendicitis or any other dysfunction of the kidney. We bless God that You alone made the body and every function thereof. I recognize that I cannot pray for every function and attribute of baby's body, because what You have created within the human body is beyond what the human mind can comprehend. However, we do not lean on our own knowledge, nor the knowledge and understanding of scientist and doctors alone, but we trust and depend on the all-knowing God. "In God have I put my trust: I will not be afraid what man can do unto me" (Psalm 56:11, KJV). God, I love You. In Jesus' name. Amen.

Day 6

God, thank You for being an all-knowing God. We bless You for Your power and might in our lives. Please continue to look upon baby and bless baby. As our baby grows and develops in my womb, guide the maturation of baby's intestines. Thank You that a loop of baby's growing intestines is now connected to the umbilical cord. Thank You that the umbilical cord is able to carry oxygen and nutrients to and from baby. Please bless the intestines to continue to grow and mature properly as the intestines are properly placed within baby's body (in time) and function with godly perfection. Bless baby to receive the proper amount of oxygen and nutrients daily. Help me to eat properly so that my baby is blessed and never harmed by my eating habits. Thank You that baby is properly growing and gaining strength each day within my womb. Please bless my womb to be a safe and comfortable habitat for baby until he or she has fully developed at forty weeks (or more). Please fulfill the number of days required for baby to be within my womb. "I will fulfill the number of your days" (Exodus 23:26, ESV). In Jesus' name. Amen.

Day 7

God, thank You for joy and peace. You have been gracious in our lives. I cannot say it enough—there is no way to overstate Your graciousness to us. "But by the grace of God I am what I am: and His grace which was bestowed upon me was not in vain; but I laboured more abundantly than they all: yet not I, but the grace of God which was with me" (1 Corinthians 15:10 KJV). Please continue to bless us with Your grace. I pray that You continue to increase my joy, peace, and happiness daily. Thank You for blessing baby's teeth as they begin to form and develop beneath baby's gums. We thank you that baby's teeth will grow in healthy, straight, strong, and precisely placed within the mouth. Please bless our baby's teething period. I pray that baby's teething is not a strenuous or unpleasant period for baby, me, or my husband. Even as baby grows and begins to lose teeth, I thank You that losing teeth is not an unpleasant experience for my baby. When baby's adult teeth grow in, allow baby's adult teeth to also be healthy, straight, strong, and precisely placed within baby's mouth. Help me to receive enough calcium to properly nourish baby's teeth and bones. Please bless baby's gums to be healthy and never infected or cause undue problems for baby. In Jesus' name. Amen.

My Letter to Baby: Date: _____

Week 8

"For by him were all things created, that are in heaven, and that are in earth, visible and invisible, whether they be thrones, or dominions, or principalities, or powers: all things were created by him, and for him: And he is before all things, and by him all things consist" (Colossians 1:16–17, KJV).

Day 1

God, thank You for Your amazing grace. As we enter a new week of growth and development for both me and my baby, we thank You for every moment of nausea, hunger, and fatigue. Although time-consuming and often inconvenient, nausea, hunger, and fatigue reassure me of the promise You have entrusted me with. I pray that as baby's cartilage and bones begin to form, You would provide enough nutrients and calcium for baby's growth. Thank You that baby's bones and cartilage are strong and sturdy. I thank You that baby is not easily injured—physically or spiritually. Please bless baby to grow tall (or the height that You have predestined baby to be), with proportional legs, arms, hands, fingers, feet, and toes. Thank You that baby is successful in each athletic pursuit and extracurricular activity that is within Your will. I know You have great plans for baby, all of which I trust You to fulfill, because "many, O LORD my God, are the wonders you have done. The things you planned for us no one can recount to You; were I to speak and tell of them, they would be too many to declare" (Psalm 40:5, NIV). Thank You that my baby is always protected by You while in the womb and outside of the womb. You, Lord, will keep baby; You will preserve baby from this generation forever (Psalm 12:7). In Jesus' name. Amen.

Day 2

God, thank You for Your everlasting love. "I have loved you with an everlasting love" (Jeremiah 31:3, NIV). As baby's eyes form, please perfect the vision of baby's eyes—spiritually and physically. I thank You that baby always finds grace in your eyes, as Noah did (Genesis 6:8). As baby seeks and discovers new things, above all things sought, I pray that baby seeks the kingdom of God and lives righteously, and You will give baby everything they need (Matthew 6:33). In Jesus' name. Amen.

Day 3

God, thank You for never failing. You are a wonderful God, and we appreciate Your loving kindness towards us. Thank You for blessing baby's growth daily. Today, as baby reaches nearly an inch in length and a gram in weight, please continue to bless the growth of baby, from the crown of baby's head to the soles of baby's feet. Thank you for perfecting baby's breathing tubes, which extend from baby's throat to the branches of baby's developing lungs. We praise You that baby never has breathing problems, asthma, or lung complications. When baby is down, sick, or discombobulated, please breathe a fresh breath of life into baby (even as an adult). Thank You that in Your time, You will breathe on baby, and baby will receive the Holy Ghost (John 20:22). In Jesus' name. Amen.

Day 4

God, thank You for always walking with us and before us. You have consistently cleared the path before us and made our way straight (Luke 3:5). Please let the blessings of God be upon the development and maturation of baby's tongue. We recognize that death and life are in the power of the tongue (Proverbs 18:21); direct baby's tongue to speak life. I thank You that baby is able to speak well, even at an early age, and utilizes this gift to speak well of You, Lord. Help us to properly raise baby so that baby's tongue is able to confess at an early age that Jesus Christ is Lord (Philippians 2:11). In Jesus' name. Amen.

Day 5

God, we thank You for being the only wise God (Jude 1:25). We recognize that we do not know everything, nor are we able to pray for everything as we should; however, You have made it possible for the Spirit himself to intercede for us with groans that words cannot express (Romans 8:26). I pray that as baby continues to mature and develop within my womb, You would bless and anoint each step of baby's progression. Please enable the intestines to properly move out of the umbilical cord into baby's abdomen. Thank You that the intestines and all related attributes are properly formed, correctly positioned, and function perfectly. In Jesus' name. Amen.

Day 6

God, thank You that we can stand on Your Word, for You have held Your Word above Your beautiful name (Psalm 138:2). You have removed fear from our hearts and minds and shown us the salvation of the Lord (Exodus 14:13). We pray that You would continue to bless and direct the development of baby's fingers and toes. As baby's fingers and toes grow from the hands and feet, we thank You for perfecting baby's fingers, toes, hands, and feet. Please, let the beauty of the Lord our God be upon us and establish the work of baby's hands (Psalm 90:17). In Jesus' name. Amen.

Day 7

God, we are thankful that there is no limit to Your goodness or Your power. Our Lord is great and of great power: his understanding is infinite (Psalm 147:5). As baby's brain continues to mature and develop, we thank You for blessing each of baby's billions of nerve cells. Please bless the nerve cells as they branch out to connect with other nerve cells to form neural pathways. We thank You for perfecting the number of brain cells, the connecting pathways, and the function of the neural pathways. We honor You for overseeing every activity of baby as he or she moves and shifts within me. I pray that You would direct my actions and reactions so that I provide a safe and comfortable habitation for baby. In Jesus' name, Amen.

My Letter to Baby: Date: _____

Week 9

"The LORD shall increase you more and more, you and your children" (Psalm 115:14, KJV).

Day 1

God, I am amazed at Your work, and I thank You for the opportunity to carry life in my womb. We cannot deny that Your works are great and wonderful (Revelation 15:3). As baby's heart completes the process of dividing into four chambers, we pray that each chamber is properly formed and perfectly functional. Thank You that the valves now forming between the chambers of baby's heart are wonderfully made. We thank You that the leaflets of baby's valves open and close fully with perfect timing to allow blood to flow in the proper direction to the proper location(s) of baby's heart. Thank You that baby never suffers from a defective heart valve or infection due to the activity of the heart valve(s). Additionally, Lord, please give baby a heart to know You. "I will give them a heart to know me, that I am the LORD. They will be my people, and I will be their God, for they will return to me with all their heart" (Jeremiah 24:7, NIV). In Jesus' name. Amen.

Day 2

God, thank You for being our provider—Jehovah-Jireh—for it is You who supplies all our need according to Your glorious riches in Christ Jesus (Philippians 4:19). Please continue to provide proper nutrients and oxygen to baby for healthy growth and development. Thank You for continuing to bless the growth and formation of baby's teeth beneath the gums. Although it will be a while before baby may utilize these teeth, these weeks remain a very critical time of teeth growth and formation. Please bless baby's teeth to remain healthy and grow in properly. When baby's teeth grow in, please allow this to be a fun and painless transition for baby. Thank You that baby will not fight against brushing, flossing, and maintaining good oral hygiene. Please guide me during the teething transition—and *all* transitions. Thank You that Your Word says You will guide us always (Isaiah 58:11). In Jesus' name. Amen.

Day 3

God, thank You that You have given us authority to overcome all the power of the enemy, and nothing shall by any means harm us (Luke 10:19). Great and mighty are You, Lord, our great and matchless King! We pray today that as our baby continues to grow and mature in my womb, You would continue to bless baby's organs, muscles, and nerves. We recognize that baby's organs, muscles, and nerves have begun to operate at an even greater capacity. We ask that You would bestow Your strength upon baby as his or her organs, muscles, and nerves perform new activities and realize new capabilities. Thank You that as baby grows from infancy to adulthood, his or her health, strength (physical and spiritual), and abilities are never bound by earthly confines, because You are baby's strength every morning and salvation in time of distress! (Isaiah 33:2) In Jesus' name. Amen.

Week 9

Day 4

God, thank You for being a very present (right now) help to us (Psalm 46:1). We recognize that our knowledge is limited, and baby's current stage of growth may be ahead of our current awareness; therefore, we ask that You would meet baby's current needs. As baby's eyes form and develop, thank You for continuing to bless and perfect baby's eyesight. I pray that the muscles that control baby's eye movements are strong. Thank You that the color and shape of baby's eyes compliment the wonderful personality You have graced baby to possess. As baby grows and matures outside the womb, thank You that in time of frustration, pain, and sorrow, You comfort baby and wipe away the tears from his or her eyes (Revelation 21:4). In Jesus' name. Amen.

Day 5

God, thank You for allowing us to put our trust in You. Lord, it comforts me to know that no matter how I feel or how things look outwardly, I can trust in Your plan for me. In all honesty, I don't feel pregnant every day, and there are times that this makes me nervous; but when I recall Your goodness in my life and my history with You, I have hope (Lamentations 3:2). Please continue to bestow Your blessings on baby as the earlobes, mouth, nose, and nostrils form and become even more distinct. Thank You for being the master Creator. Please continue to perfect the formation of each of baby's features. We thank You for blessing the function, development, and esthetics of baby's earlobes, mouth, nose, and nostrils. I pray that baby's mouth is used for the edification of Your name, O Lord (1 Corinthians 14:26). In Jesus' name. Amen.

Day 6

God, thank You for renewing our youth and our strength (Psalm 103:5, Isaiah 40:31). You have carefully created the placenta to supply the fetus with oxygen and food and to allow the fetal waste to be disposed via the maternal kidneys. Your handiwork is amazing. You have designed life to grow within me, and you have perfected a habitat of nourishment and growth for the life of my baby. Please perfect the operations of the placenta. Thank You that the placenta is producing the right type and correct amount of fluid and hormones for me and the baby. In Jesus' name. Amen.

Day 7

God, thank You that Your faithfulness endures to all generations (Psalm 119: 90). Thank You for the new generation that currently resides within me. Please help me to provide a happy and healthy environment for baby as he or she begins a time of rapid weight gain. Help me to eat the proper foods, maintain proper exercise, and obtain plenty of rest. Thank You that baby and I gain the right amount of weight at the right times. We thank You that You continue to bestow Your blessings on baby's growth and maturation—now and always. O Lord, when I have not provided the proper nourishment to baby, please nourish baby from heaven. We know that, like Daniel, this baby will be healthy, wise, and strong (Daniel 1:15–20). In Jesus' name. Amen.

My Letter to Baby:

Date: _____

Week 10

"Fix these words of mine in your hearts and minds; tie them as symbols on your hands and bind them on your foreheads. Teach them to your children, talking about them when you sit at home and when you walk along the road, when you lie down and when you get up" (Deuteronomy 11:18–19, NIV).

Day 1

God, thank You that You are a strategic God and that You have planned out our lives for our good and for Your glory. "Many, O LORD my God, are the wonders you have done. The things You planned for us no one can recount to You; were I to speak and tell of them, they would be too many to declare" (Psalm 40:5, NIV). We appreciate You, Lord. Thank You for keeping Your promises. Thank You that no one can thwart the plan You have for us and our baby. Thank You for caring for baby as he or she has grown into a fetus. You have been faithful in the formation of baby during this critical time of development. As we move into a new period of rapid growth and maturation for baby, please continue to take care to guide and bless each step of baby's growth. Your Word says that You will take care of the growth of our seed (2 Corinthians 9:10). This baby is our seed; please take care of baby's growth. In Jesus' name. Amen.

Day 2

God, thank You for creating ways to bless us. Like Mary, "My soul doth magnify the Lord!" (Luke 1:46). We pray Your blessings on baby as he or she continues to grow and mature in my womb. Baby's brain is developing more rapidly each day. Thank You for perfecting baby's brain and all components thereof. We thank You that every aspect of this highly complex organ that You have designed is created flawlessly within baby. Please direct me to read and talk to baby to assist in baby's development. Give me words to say and tell me how to speak in a manner that pleases you first and that blesses baby. Thank You that my mouth utters wisdom and my tongue speaks what is just (Psalm 37:30)—for baby's good and for Your glory! In Jesus' name, Amen.

Day 3

God, thank You, for no one can contend with You (1 Samuel 2:10). Your promises of protection (2 Samuel 22:3), provision (Psalm 144:13), and perfection (Psalm 18:32) are sure. As baby's eyes begin to develop, thank You for perfecting the formation and progression of baby's eye development. How You have formed every amazing feature of the eye is to be marveled. Among the many elements which are forming within baby's eyes, You have created the iris to be responsible for controlling the diameter and size of baby's pupil as well as controlling the amount of light that reaches baby's retina (once You allow the baby's eyelids to open). Thank You that every aspect of baby's eyes is blessed, baby's eyesight is precise, and that baby will never suffer from any disease of the eyes or any eye abnormality. We stand on Your Word, which says, that we can ask, and it shall be given (Matthew 7:7). In Jesus' name. Amen.

Day 4

God, thank You, for what the enemy meant for evil, You made it for good (Genesis 50:20). We are forever grateful for the ways You continuously bless our lives. Thank You that baby is now kicking, stretching, and flexing. Although we cannot feel baby's movements yet, we are confident of the work You are performing within us. You have enabled baby's vital organs to form, including baby's kidneys, intestines, brain, and liver; You have blessed each stage of the vital organs' development. Thank You. We recognize that these organs are functioning and maturing daily. Please continue to guide each stage of maturation and activity. We pray that You would guide our daily diets and activities to be conducive to the healthy progression of baby's vital organs. Thank You that baby's kidneys, intestines, brain, and liver are perfected by You, and "[t]he LORD will keep [baby] free from every disease" (Deuteronomy 7:15, NIV). In Jesus' name. Amen.

Day 5

God, thank You, for heaven and earth will pass away, but Your Word will never pass away (Mark 13:31). The feeling of knowing that we can trust Your Word is awesome. We stand on the promise of Your Word to take care of every detail of our lives and baby's life, for Your Word says that You "delight in every detail of [our] lives" (Psalm 37:23, NLT). What a promise! We cannot help but be grateful that You care so much about us. Please continue to bless baby's growth and maturation in my womb. As baby's tiny fingers and toes take shape, bless the formation of every fingernail and toenail. Thank You, Lord, that baby distinctly has five fingers on each hand and five toes on each foot. Thank You that baby's feet and toes are straight, properly separated, and made perfect. We depend solely on You, for You are the God of creation (Genesis 1:1). In Jesus' name. Amen.

Day 6

God, thank You for being faithful, even when we are faithless. "If we are faithless, He will remain faithful, for He cannot disown Himself" (2 Timothy 2:13, NIV). Your greatness never ceases to amaze us—you, Lord, are better to us than we could be to ourselves. We are forever grateful. No matter what a situation appears to be, You are God, the faithful God (Deuteronomy 7:9). We are amazed at how You have enabled baby's limbs to grow and now flex. Please bless the growth and maturation of each individual bone within baby's body. Perfect every ligament, tendon, muscle, and piece of cartilage that supports and supplements baby's bones. God, we wait patiently upon You, for our expectation, our faith, and our hope is in You (Psalm 62:5). In Jesus' name. Amen.

Day 7

God, thank You that Your judgments are unsearchable and Your ways are unfathomable (Romans 11:33). We may never comprehend how mighty You are, but we thank You for being mighty in our lives. Lord, please do not allow the enemy to plague our minds with thoughts that are not of You. Calm our fears, and give us peace. You are a perfect God. You work in perfect time and in a perfect way. "He is the Rock, his works are perfect, and all his ways are just. A faithful God who does no wrong, upright and just is he" (Deuteronomy 32:4, NIV). As we near the completion of another week of gestation, we simply say, "Thank You." Please continue to bless the maturation of baby in my womb. Baby's spine is now obvious, and baby's spinal nerves are beginning to extend from the spinal cord. Thank You that baby's spine is made perfect. As the spinal nerves grow and extend to various parts of the body, please perfect every connection and operation thereof. We pray that baby never experiences a spinal cord or back injury or dysfunction. In Jesus' name. Amen.

My Letter to Baby:

Date: _____

Week 11

"Every good gift and every perfect gift is from above, and cometh down from the Father of lights, with whom is no variableness, neither shadow of turning" (James 1:17, KJV).

Day 1

God, thank You for being trustworthy. "God is not a man, that He should lie, Nor a son of man, that He should repent; Has He said, and will He not do it? Or has He spoken, and will He not make it good?" (Numbers 23:19, NASB) Help us to cling to the unchanging, never-failing God (Malachi 3:6). Let us be faithful to complete the vows that we have made to You. Help us to teach our baby to have integrity and to be honorable. I pray that You would bless the growth and maturation of baby's bones. Thank You that baby's bones are beginning to harden and become stronger by the day. Please bless baby with the nutrients needed for healthy, strong development. Where I fall short in providing the proper nutrients to baby, please continue to supply all the nourishment baby needs to grow and to be healthy. In Jesus' name. Amen.

Day 2

God, thank You for the opportunity to make our request known unto You, for we know that You listen to our requests, we can be sure that we have what we ask You for (1 John 5:15). Nearly all of baby's bodily structure and organs are formed and are beginning to function. Thank You for taking special care to perfectly form each of baby's parts. Please continue to bless the functionality of baby's organs and parts. As baby continues to grow and mature, please continue to keep him or her free from every disease, as Your Word promises in Deuteronomy 7:15: "The LORD will keep you free from every disease" (NIV). In Jesus' name. Amen.

Day 3

God, thank You for the opportunity to cherish this time of having baby close to me. I anxiously wait to hear baby's heartbeat, to see the next ultrasound, and even to hold my precious baby. Please help me to be anxious for nothing, but in everything, by prayer and supplication, with thanksgiving, let my requests be made known to You (Philippians 4:6). Baby's hair and nails are beginning to grow. Thank You for anointing the hair upon baby's head, and please bless baby's nails. Thank You that baby never suffers from dry scalp, hair or hair follicle disorders, or nail fungus or disease. Thank You that baby receives the proper nourishment and protein so that his or her hair and nails grow properly and remain healthy after birth. In Jesus' name. Amen.

Day 4

God, thank You for allowing us to think on things which are true, honest, just, pure, lovely, and of good report (Philippians 4:8). Lord, if there be any virtue, and if there be any praise, we shall think on these things (Philippians 4:8). So often, we unintentionally and unnecessarily add grief and heartache to our lives. Please help us to meditate on Your goodness, Lord, and the many blessings You have bestowed upon our lives. Make our hearts merry with laughter, for "a merry heart maketh a cheerful countenance" (Proverbs 15:13). I pray that both baby and I will continuously have a cheerful countenance, "for the Mighty One has done great things for me—Holy is his name" (Luke 1:49, NIV). As baby's genitals take on characteristics according to his or her gender, please bless the genitals to grow and mature properly. Thank You that baby never suffers from any disorder, dysfunction, deformities, or disease of the genitals. In Jesus' name. Amen.

Day 5

God, thank You for being the love of my life. "To love him with all your heart, with all your understanding and with all your strength, and to love your neighbor as yourself is more important than all burnt offerings and sacrifices" (Mark 12:33, NIV). Please continue to bless baby's growth and maturation within my womb. As the amniotic fluid accumulates within the amniotic sac, please bless the liquid and all proteins, carbohydrates, lipids, phospholipids, urea, and electrolytes contained therein which support the growth of the fetus. Thank You for perfecting the amount of amniotic fluid produced by my baby and I. Allow baby to be comfortable and safely cushioned within my womb. We rebuke the preterm rupturing of the amniotic membranes and any dysfunction that may cause preterm labor. In Jesus' name. Amen.

Day 6

God, thank You for being a constant friend. "There is a friend that sticketh closer than a brother" (Proverbs 18:24, KJV). Every day, baby and I embark on a new experience. Thank You for being a friend to us as we travel this new journey. Please continue to develop the muscles in baby's intestinal walls. Perfect the intestinal wall muscles as the muscles begin to expand and contract in preparation to digest food. Bless baby's digestive tract to always properly digest food and excrete waste. Thank You in advance that baby has a great appetite for food and an even greater appetite for You, Lord, and Your Word. "O taste and see that the LORD is good: blessed is the man that trusteth in him" (Psalm 34:8, KJV). In Jesus' name. Amen.

Day 7

God, thank You for being the center of our family. "Except the LORD build the house, they labour in vain that build it" (Psalm 127:1, KJV). Wherever we have fallen short in making You the center of our family, we repent now, and we give You authority over our home. Soon, our family will begin a new life together with baby. Lord, increase our capacity for love. Please help baby's father and me to love You better each day and to love each other more and more every day (1 John 4:16). Thank you for the love You have already given us for baby; please let this love only grow and never find reason to diminish. Thank You for increasing our finances. Make provision for us to enjoy the blessings of life and to enjoy blessing others. "He who is kind to the poor lends to the LORD, and he will reward him for what he has done" (Proverbs 19:17, NIV). In Jesus' name. Amen.

My Letter to Baby: Date: _____

Week 12

"Children are a gift from the LORD; they are a reward from him" (Psalm 127:3, NLT).

Day 1

God, thank You for creating ways to bless us—Your children. Lord, just like You created manna in the wilderness for the Israelites (Exodus 16:35), You have created ways to keep Your promises to us. We give You thanks! With the daily maturation and development of baby, You have set in motion the development of baby's vocal cords. We pray that baby gives You praise with the voice You are producing within his or her vocal cords. Thank You, Lord, for perfecting the formation of baby's vocal cords, and thank You for the voice You have purposed for baby. We pray that baby never experiences a vocal cord problem or disorder. Lord, when baby calls you, please hear his or her voice, and let Your ears be attentive to their supplications (Psalm 130:2). In Jesus' name. Amen.

Day 2

God, we worship and adore You! (1 Chronicles 16:29) Regardless of our surroundings and the happenings of current events, help us to keep our eyes fixed on You. "Let us fix our eyes on Jesus, the author and perfecter of our faith" (Hebrews 12:2, NIV). As baby's eyes continue to mature and move into place, please continue to bless the development and maturation of the eyes. Although we are unsure of baby's eye color and we understand that our baby's eye color will be determined by multiple genes, we pray that baby's eye color is consistent with Your will. Thank You that baby's eye shape, size, position, and vision are perfect according to Your plan, for we know that Your work is perfect (Deuteronomy 32:4). In Jesus' name. Amen.

Day 3

God, thank You that we do not have to look to other places for satisfaction, but that we can find our satisfaction in You. "My people shall be satisfied with my goodness, said the LORD" (Jeremiah 31:14, KJV). Many attributes of baby are changing daily. Lord, please be in control of every shift, movement, and change that is taking place on or within baby. As baby's ears shift into place, thank You that the final destination of baby's ears is in the perfect place, with perfect shape, and working in perfect order. We thank You that "faith cometh by hearing, and hearing by the word of God" (Romans 10:17). Please help us to hear and be obedient to Your Word so that we may properly impart listening and obedience to baby. "I long to see you so that I may impart to you some spiritual gift to make you strong" (Romans 1:11, NIV). In Jesus' name. Amen.

Day 4

God, thank You for establishing an everlasting covenant with us (Ezekiel 16:60). Your covenant with us was forever instated "through the offering of the body of Jesus Christ once for all" (Hebrews 10:10, NKJV). Thank You for being the ultimate sacrifice (Hebrews 9:12). As You direct the happenings within my womb, please direct baby's intestines to move into their proper positions within baby's body. Bless and perfect all activity of baby's intestines while within me and after birth. Help us to teach baby about the wonderful sacrifice You gave of Your one and only begotten son (1 John 4:9) so that we may have eternal life. "God has given us eternal life, and this life is in His Son" (1 John 5:11, NIV). In Jesus' name. Amen.

Day 5

God, thank You that there is no one like You. Who is like the Lord? *Nobody!* "There is no one holy like the LORD; there is no one besides you; there is no Rock like our God" (1 Samuel 2:2, NIV). "Who among the gods is like you, O LORD? Who is like you—majestic in holiness, awesome in glory, working wonders?" (Exodus 15:11, NIV) Many parts of baby's anatomy are developing and beginning to function. As baby's liver begins to function, please bless the liver to always be healthy. Thank You that baby's liver is cleaning the blood, properly storing nutrients, and strategically producing the biochemicals necessary for baby's digestion. Please protect baby's liver from liver disease, cancer, or any sickness that causes liver complications. May the Lord always bless and keep our baby (Numbers 6:24). In Jesus' name. Amen.

Week 12

Day 6

God, thank You that we can rejoice, for You have made us glad! "I will be glad and rejoice in your love, for you saw my affliction and knew the anguish of my soul" (Psalm 31:7, NIV). Lord, You never leave us in our anguish, but You have delivered us, and You will continue to deliver us! (2 Corinthians 1:10) As baby's pancreas begins to produce insulin, please bless baby's pancreas so that the pancreas will always produce enough insulin, and bless baby's body so that it will always respond properly to the insulin produced by baby's pancreas. Thank You that baby's pancreas produces the proper amount and type of hormones and enzymes for the wellbeing of baby in utero and after birth. We pray that baby's pancreas is always healthy and never suffers from any form of sickness or disease. In Jesus' name. Amen.

Day 7

God, thank You for abundant life. "I am come that they might have life, and that they might have it more abundantly" (John 10:10, KJV). Thank You for the new life that resides within me. Baby is growing in length and weight every day. Although I cannot see the changes in baby's body, I am noticing changes in my own body. Please help me to always be confident in the woman You have made me to be. Help me to embrace the changes in my body. Additionally, help my husband to embrace the changes in my body and always love me as Christ loved the church. "Husbands, love your wives, just as Christ loved the church and gave himself up for her" (Ephesians 5:25, NIV). Please manage and correct any negative changes in my personality. Guide me to always portray the fruit of the Spirit—love, joy, peace, longsuffering, gentleness, goodness, faith, meekness, and temperance (Galatians 5:22–23). Bless every inch and ounce of the baby that grows inside me. Anoint me to be the mother You have undeniably chosen for my baby. In Jesus' name. Amen.

My Letter to Baby:

Date: _____

Week 13

"For whatsoever is born of God overcometh the world: and this is the victory that overcometh the world, even our faith" (1 John 5:4, KJV).

Day 1

God, thank You, for "surely the LORD has done great things" (Joel 2:21, NIV). You are a marvelous God, and no matter what the situation appears to be, You remain in control. Baby is beginning to practice inhaling and exhaling. Please perfect baby's breathing in utero and after birth. Bless my baby so he or she never has to experience tracheal intubation or any breathing assistance. Please bless each anatomical feature of baby's respiratory system. Thank You that baby's respiratory system is made perfectly and operates flawlessly. We pray now for any children who are experiencing problems with their respiratory systems. Please bless them to be healed and delivered from the problem that plagues them, for by Your stripes, we are healed (1 Peter 2:24). In Jesus' name. Amen.

Day 2

God, thank You that where two or three are gathered in Your name, You are in their midst (Matthew 18:20). My baby and I are two who are gathered, and we thank You that You are in the midst of us as we ask Your blessing on baby's father. As my husband works really hard each day, please take care of his heart, mind, soul, and body. Bless him to always have a heart to worship Jesus and a heart to love his family. Please let the blessing of the Lord be upon him to perfect all the work of his hands. "And let the beauty of the LORD our God be upon us: and establish thou the work of our hands upon us; yea, the work of our hands establish thou it" (Psalm 90:17, KJV). As he continues to work hard to bless and provide for our family, please continue to remove worldly limitations from him (Deuteronomy 28:12–13). Thank You for the plan You have set in motion for baby's father and our family, and thank You for the strategic execution of Your plan! In Jesus' name. Amen.

Day 3

God, thank You that we can sing for joy at the works of Your hands. "For thou, LORD, hast made me glad through Thy work: I will triumph in the works of Thy hands" (Psalm 92:4, KJV). The work You are performing in us through baby has made us glad. I pray for mothers who have experienced or will experience preterm births. Please bless their babies to become healthy and strong. Restore to perfect health any issue or illness a premature baby experiences, and restore the mother completely—mentally and physically. Please protect me from all causes of preterm birth—known and unknown, detected and undetected. Thank You that preterm premature rupture of the membranes or cervical insufficiency is never a problem for me. I am grateful to know that You will complete the work You have begun in me. Your Word says, "Will I by whom the birth was started, not make it complete? says the Lord" (Isaiah 66:9, BBE). In Jesus' name. Amen.

Day 4

God, thank You that there is no limit to the love You have for us; please increase our capacity to love. "May the Lord make your love increase and overflow for each other and for everyone else, just as ours does for you" (1 Thessalonians 3:12, NIV). Baby is maturing more and more each day. You have blessed baby's hands to become more functional and active. Thank You that baby's hands are blessed. May the favor of the Lord our God rest upon my baby; please always establish the work of baby's hands (Psalm 90:17). In Jesus' name. Amen.

Day 5

God, thank You that nothing compares to the promise we have in You. "For if the inheritance depends on the law, then it no longer depends on a promise; but God in His grace gave it to Abraham through a promise" (Galatians 3:18, NIV). Naturally speaking, baby is receiving all nourishment from my placenta. Spiritually speaking, baby and I need You to continuously nourish our bodies, minds, and souls—now and after baby is born. Help me to continuously seek and obey Your Word and to trust in Your promise to our family. In Jesus' name, Amen.

Day 6

God, thank You that no matter what we face in life, Your Word has the answer. "In Him was life, and that life was the light of men" (John 1:4, NIV). My baby's eyes and ears are continuing to move into place and develop. You have meticulously designed the eyes and ears of man. Man can neither recreate nor copy what You have created. Perfect Your creation. Where my body falls short in being the perfect host for baby's developing body, please replenish me. In Jesus' name. Amen.

Day 7

God, thank You for never abandoning us. "The LORD himself goes before you and will be with you; He will never leave you nor forsake you. Do not be afraid; do not be discouraged" (Deuteronomy 31:8, NIV). I grow more excited each day to know that my baby is maturing within me. As baby's neck elongates and gets stronger, please bless every aspect of his or her neck. Bless baby's neck to properly support the weight of the head. Allow baby's neck to properly carry sensory and motor information from the brain to the rest of the body. Please perfect the movement and flexibility of baby's neck. In Jesus' name. Amen.

My Letter to Baby:

Date: _____

Week 14

"Even the youths shall faint and be weary, and the young men shall utterly fall: But they that wait upon the LORD shall renew their strength; they shall mount up with wings as eagles; they shall run, and not be weary; and they shall walk, and not faint" (Isaiah 40:30–31, KJV).

Day 1

God, thank You that Your Word runneth very swiftly (Psalm 147:15); therefore, we can speak Your Word in prayer from our current location and trust that Your Word "runneth very swiftly" to a target location and performs that which is spoken. For that reason, together, my baby and I pray for the health and strength of each baby in every neonatal intensive care unit (NICU). You are an omnipresent God; please reveal yourself in every NICU. Please touch and heal each problem. Help the doctors, nurses, and hospital staff to work diligently. Give each of them understanding of what to do and how to perform the tasks which have been laid before them. There will be tasks that the doctors and nursing staff cannot handle; please show them Your greatness. Let the babies, families, doctors, and nurses see Your benefits towards us (Psalm 103:3–5). Thank You that our baby never has to be admitted to a NICU. As baby's pain senses mature in utero, please keep him or her safe from all hurt, harm, and danger (Psalm 91:10–11). In Jesus' name. Amen.

Week 14

Day 2

God, thank You for being all that we need. "Command those who are rich in this present world not to be arrogant nor to put their hope in wealth, which is so uncertain, but to put their hope in God, who richly provides us with everything for our enjoyment" (1 Timothy 6:17, NIV). With every passing day, we grow more grateful for Your love and provision to us. Please continue to watch over my baby as he or she grows and matures within me. Baby's thyroid gland has matured, and baby is now producing hormones that will be utilized throughout his or her life. Please bless each hormone to properly perform the task that has been assigned by You. As baby's hormones travel through the blood stream, thank you that the hormones appropriately affect baby's growth and development, metabolism, and temperament. At Your ordained time (when my child is married), bless his or her sexual and reproductive hormones to also work appropriately. In Jesus' name. Amen.

Day 3

God, thank You for being a promise-keeper. "The Lord is not slack concerning his promise" (2 Peter 3:9, KJV). You will never rescind Your promise to us; help us to be true to our commitments to You. At this point of my baby's development, either the prostate gland is developing or the ovaries are moving from the abdomen to the pelvis. Please bless baby's prostate or ovaries to progress with perfection. Allow baby's prostate or ovaries to always operate properly. Thank You that cancer never infests baby's prostate or ovaries, for You, Lord, have promised to keep us free from every disease (Deuteronomy 7:15). In Jesus' name. Amen.

Day 4

God, thank You that Your Word is truth! "For this cause also thank we God without ceasing, because, when you received the word of God which you heard of us, you received it not as the word of men, but as it is in truth, the word of God, which effectually works also in you that believe" (1 Thessalonians 2:13, KJV). We depend on Your truth to work in us and for us daily. You have my permission to allow Your truth for peace (2 Thessalonians 3:16), protection (Psalm 3:3), and provision (Genesis 22:14) to work in my life daily. As baby's brain continues to grow and develop, help me to desire and eat foods that will bless the development of baby's brain. Bless every brain impulse to operate in its God-ordained assignment. In Jesus' name. Amen.

Day 5

God, we are thankful that we can depend on Your flawless Word. "Every word of God is flawless; he is a shield to those who take refuge in him" (Proverbs 30:5, NIV). Please help our family to continuously look to Your Word and seek Your face so that we may hear from You and be led by You, O Lord. Continue to watch over the maturation of baby's body. Baby's lanugo is growing to protect the skin, baby's bones are growing harder and stronger each day, and even unique fingerprints have developed and become apparent on baby. Bless every aspect of baby's growth. We are excited to know that baby's physical identity becomes more obvious every day; however, help our baby to always find his or her total identity (body, mind, and soul) in You (1 Peter 2:9–10). In Jesus' name. Amen.

Day 6

God, thank You for choosing us. "You did not choose me, but I chose you and appointed you to go and bear fruit—fruit that will last. Then the Father will give you whatever you ask in my name" (John 15:16, NIV). Help us to live lives that are full and beneficial to the kingdom of God. Help us to teach our baby to not be selfish with the gifts and callings You have entrusted in us. Increase my strength, and perfect my health as I provide a habitat for the beautiful being inside me. My baby's kidneys are producing urine that releases into the amniotic fluid around him or her; please perfect this process and the function of baby's kidneys—now and always. In Jesus' name. Amen.

Day 7

God, thank You that Your greatness is unsearchable (Psalm 145:3). We could never comprehend how great You are, O Lord; nor can we measure Your love toward us. For this, we are truly grateful. We appreciate You, God. There is no sacrifice that can ever repay You for Your unsearchable greatness or immeasurable love, nor have You desired such a sacrifice (Psalm 51:16). You have simply asked us to have "a broken spirit; a broken and a contrite heart" (Psalm 51:17). As baby's father and I go through the physical, mental, and spiritual changes associated with bringing a new life into the world, please help us exude the broken spirits and broken, contrite hearts which You have requested of us. Replenish my health and strength so that I may be a suitable helper (Exodus 15:26, Psalm 27:14, Genesis 2:18). Establish the work of my husband's hands (Psalm 90:17) so that he may be a great provider. Thank You for the blessing of Psalm 112 upon my husband; please do not withhold any good thing from him (Psalm 84:11). In Jesus' name. Amen.

My Letter to Baby: Date: _____

Week 15

"He hath blessed thy children within thee" (Psalm 147:13, KJV).

Day 1

God, thank You for the *victory!* Although things often look seemingly impossible, we are grateful to say, "But thanks be to God, which giveth us the victory through our Lord Jesus Christ" (1 Corinthians 15:57, KJV). God, You are simply amazing. We are thankful that no matter what the situation around us appears to be, You will bypass what is ordinary to perform the extraordinary for us and through us. "God did extraordinary miracles through Paul" (Acts 19:11, NIV). As baby's middle ear bones begin to harden and the ear continues to fully develop, we pray that You will perfect the development of baby's ears and baby's physical and spiritual hearing capacity. Protect baby's ears from any health problems or injury. Please give baby, my husband, and myself an ear to hear what the Lord says. We recognize that if we can hear You during times of trouble and decision-making, performing tasks and making decisions Your way will save us time, money, and heartache. Additionally, help us all to hear and say what You would have us to say so that men, women, and children may come to know You and love You better (Ezekiel 3:27). In Jesus' name. Amen.

Day 2

God, thank You for being incredible! "I also pray that you will understand the incredible greatness of God's power for us who believe him" (Ephesians 1:19, NLT). In Your marvelous design for life in utero, You have provided the means for amniotic fluid to move through baby's nose and upper respiratory tract so that baby's primitive air sacs, within the lungs, will grow and properly develop. Thank You for blessing baby to have and produce plenty of amniotic fluid to aid in the task of developing the air sacs. Thank You that the amniotic fluid is moving with precision and perfection to and through the appropriate places within baby's body. We thank You that baby's nose, respiratory tract, and lungs are made perfect and operate with perfection. In Jesus' name. Amen.

Day 3

God, thank You that we may come boldly unto the throne of grace. "Let us therefore come boldly unto the throne of grace, that we may obtain mercy, and find grace to help in time of need" (Hebrews 4:16, KJV). Please continue to be with us and bless baby's growth and development. Bless baby's limbs as they grow to perfect proportion. Thank You that all of baby's joints and limbs are moving properly and working in perfect order. I anticipate soon being able to feel my baby's movement consistently. Please bless each movement to be comforting and pleasant. Bless baby to have room to grow and mature properly within me. Lord, when I cannot feel my baby moving, help me to take comfort in knowing that he who began a good work in me will carry it on to completion (Philippians 1:6). In Jesus' name. Amen.

Day 4

God, thank You that no matter where we are in life—mountain top (great times) or valley (hard times)—You hear us and will do awesome works on our behalf. "Come and see what God has done, how awesome his works in man's behalf!" (Psalm 66:5, NIV) Thank You for the work You have already done in our baby. You have carefully designed and set into motion the development of baby's eyes, and although baby's eyelids are still fused shut, You have activated baby's eye senses. As baby's eyes progress in development, please continue to perfect baby's eyesight, eye motion, and all features and characteristics associated with the eyes. Your word says that You have "blessed thy children within thee" (Psalm 147:13, KJV); we depend on the promises of Your Word. In Jesus' name. Amen.

Day 5

God, we come to You with thanksgiving in our hearts. "Enter into his gates with thanksgiving, and into his courts with praise: be thankful unto him, and bless his name" (Psalm 100:4, KJV). Each day, baby is maturing, learning, gaining strength, and developing more senses. As baby's hearing becomes more sensitive, please guide my words and the words of those around me so that baby hears positive and uplifting words. I pray that the music I play and sing gratifies You, Lord, and contributes to the positive development of baby and his or her hearing senses. I pray that the loud noises around me are minimized so that baby is not unduly startled or made uncomfortable. Thank You, Lord, that baby's hearing is perfect and never negatively compromised. In Jesus' name. Amen.

Day 6

God, thank You for being "I AM that I AM" (Exodus 3:14), which tells me You are whatever I need You to be. I ask that You be my keeper—keep my mind attentive to the things of God. Help me never to lose focus on becoming a better Christian, wife, and mommy. Bless baby's heart as it continues to grow and mature daily. Please continue to perfect baby's heart as it quickly pumps in preparation for the large volume of blood it will pump when baby is born. Thank You that while baby is in my uterus, the ductus arteriosus and foramen ovale (blood-flow routes) of baby's heart are working properly to allow blood to flow to the required areas within baby. When baby is born, thank You that the ductus arteriosus and foramen ovale properly close and that baby's heart and circulatory system operate with perfection. In Jesus' name. Amen.

Day 7

God, thank You that with You, we shall do valiantly (Psalm 108:13). With You, we shall do valiantly in childbirth, child care, child-rearing, child-nurturing, and child correction. Please order our steps so that we may live each day—now and when baby arrives—in a way that is pleasing and acceptable to You. "Order my steps in Thy word: and let not any iniquity have dominion over me" (Psalm 119:133, KJV). Baby is growing. Baby's bones are getting harder. Baby's muscles are developing. My baby is getting stronger by the day. Please bless baby to receive enough calcium so that the skeleton will grow and mature properly. Allow baby's muscles to receive the nutrients needed to grow and become stronger. Additionally, please bless baby's skin to continue to grow and mature in accordance with Your design for baby. In Jesus' name. Amen.

My Letter to Baby: Date: _____

Week 16

"Love is patient, love is kind. It does not envy, it does not boast, it is not proud. It is not rude, it is not self-seeking, it is not easily angered, it keeps no record of wrongs" (1 Corinthians 13:4–5, NIV).

Day 1

God, thank You for keeping no record of wrongs (1 Corinthians 13:5). Please help me to portray the characteristics of love that You have described in 1 Corinthians 13:4–5 to my husband, baby, and family. Every day brings a new task and assignment. Help me be true to the responsibilities You have assigned to me, despite any conflicts. Let me never be detoured from Your will by the complications of life, people, and things. "Teach me to do thy will; for thou art my God: thy Spirit is good; lead me into the land of uprightness" (Psalm 143:10, KJV). We are thankful You have brought us to sixteen weeks of pregnancy. Please continue to bless baby's growth. Fat is beginning to form beneath baby's skin. Thank You for blessing baby with the right amount of fat in utero and after he or she is born. Thank you that our baby is well insulated within me and is properly growing on Your schedule for baby. In Jesus' name. Amen.

Day 2

God, thank You for allowing me to grow in You as my baby grows within me. "As newborn babes, desire the sincere milk of the word, that ye may grow thereby" (1 Peter 2:2). I am excited to know baby is growing inside of me. I do not know baby's exact dimensions, but I trust that You are perfecting baby's length and weight. I cannot see or feel every move, hiccup, blink, swallow, or sucking activity; but by faith, I know that these activities are occurring. "Now faith is the substance of things hoped for, the evidence of things not seen" (Hebrews 11:1, KJV). Thank You, Lord, for the measure of faith You have given us (Romans 12:3). Please increase our desire to know You, and allow our faith in You to also be increased. In Jesus' name. Amen.

Day 3

God, thank You for being attentive to our prayers. "Now, my God, may your eyes be open and your ears attentive to the prayers offered in this place" (2 Chronicles 6:40, NIV). Each day, we grow more enthused and amazed by the work You are performing in our baby. Baby is beginning to breathe—essentially underwater. Your design for life is amazing. As baby breathes in amniotic fluid, we pray that baby is breathing the proper amount of amniotic fluid. Please bless baby's lungs to develop and grow perfectly. Thank You that baby does not experience any lung or respiratory complications. Lord, thank You that Your perfect breath gives our baby life (Job 33:4). In Jesus' name. Amen.

Day 4

God, thank You for sending people into our lives with encouraging words and special acts of kindness. Please bless each person who has said a prayer, spoken a kind word, or performed a sweet action to bless us (Genesis 12:3). Help my husband, my baby, and me to be thankful, compassionate, and generous to others. Although we cannot repay You, Lord, for all Your benefits towards us, help us to love You first and love our neighbor as ourselves, for this is greater than any burnt offering or sacrifice (Mark 12:33). Please bless baby's physical heart to be strong and to handle all that You have planned for our baby to do and accomplish. Additionally, please grant each of us a heart like Yours, Lord. Let the things that break Your heart break our hearts. Give us the mind of Christ (1 Corinthians 2:16) so that we may work together to fix that which causes Your heart to break. In Jesus' name. Amen.

Day 5

God, thank You that neither You nor Your Word are stagnant, but very alive and active. "For the word of God is living and active" (Hebrews 4:12, NIV). Please help us not to be stagnant in our walk with You, for we recognize that Your Word does not agree with those who are stagnant in spirit (Zephaniah 1:12). Please bless baby as he or she enters into a new period of growth spurts. Thank You that baby has the nourishment needed to support the growth spurt. Also, as baby's growth spurt commences, please allow us to have a spiritual growth spurt. Let us grow in You and know Your Word so that we may "be ready always to give an answer to every man that asketh [us] a reason of the hope that is in [us] with meekness and fear" (1 Peter 3:15). In Jesus' name. Amen.

Week 16

Day 6

God, thank You that our prayers are not bound by our limited knowledge and vocabulary, because "as the heavens are higher than the earth, so are [Your] ways higher than [our] ways and [Your] thoughts than [our] thoughts" (Isaiah 55:9, NIV). I am so thankful there is no limit to who or what You are to us, Lord. Thank You that no sickness or disease shall come to the dwelling of my husband, me, or our baby (Psalm 91:10). Please heal any existing sickness or disease (Luke 4:40) in me. Thank You for preventing sickness or bacteria (and any inflammation thereof) from being transmitted to my baby in utero, via my breast milk after birth, or via any other avenue. Thank You for blessing baby's paternal and maternal family to be blessed and healed of all affliction and disease. Lord, as the multitude followed You in Matthew 12:15, we follow You, and we request that You heal us all from sickness (known and unknown, diagnosed and not diagnosed), as You did for the multitude. "Great multitudes followed him, and he healed them all" (Matthew 12:15, KJV). In Jesus' name. Amen.

Day 7

God, thank You that Your timing is perfect. "For he says, 'In the time of my favor I heard you, and in the day of salvation I helped you'. I tell you, now is the time of God's favor, now is the day of salvation" (2 Corinthians 6:2, NIV). So often, we want things our way and in our time; thank You for hearing our request and responding in Your perfect time. We pray for Your continued blessings upon baby as he or she grows and develops. As the amount of blood baby's heart pumps increases each day, please bless baby's heart to properly manage the increasing volume of blood. Please forever protect and keep baby's heart. Also, perfect baby's blood vessels, as the blood vessels transport blood throughout baby's body. Allow Your blessing to be upon baby's arteries, capillaries, and veins (and all associated vessels) as they operate to carry blood away from the heart, exchange water and chemicals between the blood and tissues, and carry blood back to the heart. Thank You that baby's blood accurately reaches all necessary areas within the body. In Jesus' name. Amen.

My Letter to Baby:

Date: _____

Week 17

"Suffer the little children to come unto me, and forbid them not: for of such is the kingdom of God. And he took them up in his arms, put his hands upon them, and blessed them"
(Mark 10:14, 16 KJV).

Day 1

God, thank You that the joy of the Lord is our strength (Nehemiah 8:18). Thank You for strengthening the baby within my womb. My baby's length and weight are increasing daily. Please bless baby to continue to grow according to Your perfect plan for him or her. Although baby's eyelids are still closed tight, thank You for blessing baby's eyes to form and move perfectly. Baby's meconium—composed of intestinal epithelial cells, lanugo, mucus, swallowed amniotic fluid, bile, and water—is accumulating within the bowels. Allow the the meconium to stay within baby's bowels until after the birth. We pray against meconium aspiration syndrome or any meconium-stimulated problem. Please remove any sickness or threat of sickness from our baby's midst. "And ye shall serve the LORD your God, and he shall bless thy bread, and thy water; and I will take sickness away from the midst of thee" (Exodus 23:25, KJV). In Jesus' name. Amen.

Day 2

God, thank You for being true to the hope (confident trust with the expectation of fulfillment) we have in You. "Let us hold fast the confession of our hope without wavering, for he who promised is faithful" (Hebrews 10:23, ESV). Although only seventeen weeks into this gestational journey, we have great expectations and hope for the baby you have so graciously given us. Help us to maintain our hope in You, and help us to fulfill our promise to raise our baby in the way of the Lord. Every day, the umbilical cord is growing thicker and stronger. Please bless the blood and nutrients that travel through the umbilical cord to the baby in utero. Thank You that the umbilical cord is the perfect length, comprises sufficient arteries and veins for baby's healthy growth and maturation, and has no abnormalities that will cause fetal anomalies. I am so glad that You, Lord, are in control of the happenings of baby in my womb. My hope is in You. "May your unfailing love rest upon us, O LORD, even as we put our hope in you" (Psalm 33:22, NIV). In Jesus' name. Amen.

Day 3

God, thank You that there is no failure in You. "In everything he did he had great success, because the LORD was with him" (1 Samuel 18:14, NIV). Thank you that my husband, my baby, and I have great success in everything we do, because the Lord is with us. Lord, You have already selected the sex of the baby You have given us. If baby is a boy, please guide the growth and development of his prostate. Thank You that baby, his daddy, and no males in our family suffer from prostate cancer or any disease related to the prostate. Whether our baby is a boy or girl, please bless the gender and all anatomy and hormones thereof to be specific to baby's gender. We trust You to bless the growth and development of baby's gender anatomy, because

"God created man in his own image, in the image of God he created him; male and female He created them" (Genesis 1:27, NIV). In Jesus' name. Amen.

Day 4

God, thank You for deliverance from dangers—seen and unseen, known and unknown. "He delivereth and rescueth, and he worketh signs and wonders in heaven and in earth" (Daniel 6:27, KJV). Lord, You have carefully designed baby's skeleton to begin a transformation from cartilage to bones. However, You have strategically commanded the bones to remain flexible so that baby's journey through my birth canal is made easier. Please continue to bless the development of baby's bones. Thank You that my baby's bones and skeletal system are strong and indestructible. We pray that baby never suffers from bone diseases, irregular bone conditions, or skeletal abnormalities. Please cease and desist any hereditary bone condition that could affect baby. Lord, we trust You to keep all of baby's bones: let not one of them ever be broken (Psalm 34:20). In Jesus' name. Amen.

Day 5

God, thank You for being a constant friend. "There is a friend that sticks closer than a brother" (Proverbs 18:24, KJV). Baby is developing daily. I get excited about the idea of holding and caring for my baby. It is possible that not everyone understands my excitement or can take part in the joy I feel, but You, God, are a constant friend, and I am thankful. Baby's neck is now stronger, and baby is able to hold its head more erect. Thank you. Please continue to bless baby's growth and maturation as his or her limbs grow longer and stronger. Thank You that baby is developing and maturing at the proper rate. Regardless of my weight and size, please help me to be healthy and content. I rejoice in knowing You have made me a happy mother. "He settles the barren woman in her home as a happy mother of children. Praise the LORD" (Psalm 113:9, NIV). In Jesus' name. Amen.

Day 6

God, thank You for helping us to fix our eyes on that which is unseen, "for what is seen is temporary, but what is unseen is eternal" (2 Corinthians 4:18, NIV). Lord, help us to not be suspended by present feelings or affliction, for You have promised us a greater reward. As great as the birth of baby seems now, Your promises travel even beyond that great occasion. Even better, You are faithful to all Your promises and loving toward all You have made (Psalm 145:13). Baby's joints are now moving. Please bless baby to never suffer from joint dysfunction or inflammation. As baby's sweat glands start to develop, please bless the sweat glands to develop and operate properly. In Jesus' name. Amen.

Day 7

God, thank You that nothing can separate us from Your love. "Who shall separate us from the love of Christ? Shall trouble or hardship or persecution or famine or nakedness or danger or sword?" (Romans 8:35, NIV) Your love for us is amazing. You loved us so much, You took the time to make each of us unique. Amongst the millions of characteristics that will separate our baby from others, You have designed baby's finger and toe pads to possess distinguishing imprints. Please bless every feature of baby to be formed as set forth in Your plan for baby. Thank You for taking the time to create baby with distinctive detail; additionally, thank You for taking the time to form a plan for baby's life that is equally detailed. "Many,

O LORD my God, are the wonders you have done. The things you planned for us no one can recount to you; were I to speak and tell of them, they would be too many to declare" (Psalm 40:5, NIV). In Jesus' name. Amen.

My Letter to Baby:

Date: _____

Week 18

"Come, my children, listen to me; I will teach you the fear of the LORD" (Psalm 34:11, NIV).

Day 1

God, thank You for teaching us to depend solely on You. "My salvation and my honor depend on God; he is my mighty rock, my refuge" (Psalm 62:7, KJV). Daily, we face situations that are out of our reach and control. Help us to continue to trust You to handle every situation and issue we face—big or small. Please do not allow stress, strain, or worry to negatively affect baby. As baby continues to grow and mature, please continue to bless every aspect of baby's growth. As the vernix grows on baby's skin, thank You that the vernix—along with the lanugo—properly protects baby's skin. Allow baby's skin to always be healthy and not susceptible to allergic reactions or skin allergies. Please protect baby from all skin diseases. In Jesus' name. Amen.

Day 2

God, thank You for being our defender. "Deliver me from mine enemies, O my God: defend me from them that rise up against me" (Psalm 59:1, KJV). Please defend my baby and me from all issues that rise up against us. As my baby develops in utero, continue to manage and perfect baby's growth. Baby's alveoli (tiny air sacs) are forming in the lungs. Please bless the alveoli to form properly within baby's lungs. Thank You that baby's alveoli and lungs operate with perfection. Whenever baby is short of breath, please breathe a fresh breath of life into him or her. "He giveth to all life, and breath, and all things" (Acts 17:25, KJV). In Jesus' name. Amen.

Day 3

God, thank You for being mindful of us. "What is man, that Thou art mindful of him? and the son of man, that Thou visitest him?" (Psalm 8:4, KJV) We are grateful that You are a God that is concerned about us and that You attend to our cry. As baby's vocal cords form, please perfect the formation of the vocal cords. Help my husband and me to teach baby to sing Your praises with the vocal cords You are creating. Allow our family to utilize our voices to bless You. "I will bless the LORD at all times: His praise shall continually be in my mouth" (Psalm 34:1, KJV). Please help us to always to recognize that praise and cursing should not come from the same mouth (James 3:10–11). Thank You for protecting baby from all vocal cord dysfunction. I look forward to hearing my baby's first cry as he or she proceeds out of my womb. In Jesus' name, Amen.

Day 4

God, thank You for being attentive to our heart's desire. "You have granted him the desire of his heart and have not withheld the request of his lips" (Psalm 21:2, NIV). I am grateful that the condition of our hearts matters to You. Please continue to be attentive to the development and activity of baby's heart. Thank You that the ventricles, chambers, and all features associated with baby's heart have properly formed and are working in perfect order. Bless baby to always have a merry heart, for a merry heart doeth good, like medicine (Proverbs 17:22). In Jesus' name. Amen.

Day 5

God, thank You for Your ever-abounding peace. "Now may the Lord of peace himself give you peace at all times and in every way" (2 Thessalonians 3:16, NIV). Baby and I are growing daily. Please regulate my growth and baby's growth. Thank you that my weight gain is not too much or too little to support the health of me and my baby. Please bless my placenta to continue to grow and properly provide nourishment to baby. Continue to provide me with the proper vitamins and a healthy food regimen. Help me not to over-indulge, eat unhealthily, or partake in unhealthy activity. "Those who belong to Christ Jesus have crucified the sinful nature with its passions and desires" (Galations 5:24, NIV). In Jesus' name. Amen.

Day 6

God, thank You for being my hiding place. "You are my hiding place; you will protect me from trouble and surround me with songs of deliverance" (Psalm 32:7, NIV). Sometimes we feel the need to escape from the cares of the world. Thankfully, we can escape in

You and trust You to deliver us from things and situations which we cannot control. Thank You for having complete control over the development of baby in my womb. As baby's nerves continue to develop and mature, please bless the myelin to properly form around baby's nerves and to properly protect and insulate baby's neurons. Thank you that the myelin properly supports quick and accurate transmission of electrical current that is carrying data from one nerve cell to the next. Bless the myelin that surrounds baby's nerves to never become damaged or dysfunctional. In Jesus' name. Amen.

Day 7

God, thank You for the wonders of Your handiwork. "How many are your works, O LORD! In wisdom you made them all; the earth is full of your creatures" (Psalm 104:24, NIV). With every passing day, we grow more anxious—anxious to know baby's gender, anxious to feel baby's next kick. Thank you for taking care of baby and me. We are thankful that we can depend on You. Help us not to compare ourselves to others, nor trust what man says about us, but to trust in Your wisdom and perfect will for our lives. "It is better to take refuge in the LORD than to trust in man" (Psalm 118:8, NIV). In Jesus' name. Amen.

My Letter to Baby: *Date:* _____

Week 19

"From the lips of children and infants you have ordained praise" (Psalm 8:2, NIV).

Day 1

God, thank You for Your endless love toward us. "But from everlasting to everlasting the LORD's love is with those who fear Him, and His righteousness with their children's children" (Psalm 103:17, NIV). As baby's sensory development continues to expand, I pray that baby has perfect hearing, sight, touch, smell, and taste sensations; additionally, allow baby to sense Your presence and feel Your perfect love (Psalm 16:11, 1 John 2:5). Bless the development of baby's brain as the sections for hearing, sight, touch, smell, and taste are being designated within special areas of the brain. As baby develops the ability to hear my voice, please let my words help develop baby's brain and senses. Above all, let my words be pleasing to You. "Let the words of my mouth, and the meditation of my heart, be acceptable in thy sight, O LORD, my strength, and my redeemer" (Psalm 19:14, KJV). In Jesus' name. Amen.

Day 2

God, thank You for allowing us to cast our cares on You, for You care for us (1 Peter 5:7). I am so thankful that an almighty God is concerned for my husband, me, and our baby. Baby is continuing to rapidly grow. Thank You, Lord, for allowing baby's limbs to grow in proper proportions to each other and the rest of baby's body. Please perfect each limb and all attributes thereof. Thank You for the many parts that make up baby's body. Please allow each of baby's bodily parts to function properly and according to their godly purpose (1 Corinthians 12:12, 18). Similarly, allow baby to work within the body of Christ according to his or her godly purpose (1 Corinthians 12:27). In Jesus' name. Amen.

Day 3

God, thank You for making all things new! "And He that sat upon the throne said, Behold, I make all things new. And he said unto me, Write: for these words are true and faithful" (Revelation 21:6, KJV). We pray for each baby who is suffering from kidney problems. Please restore and rejuvenate each kidney that has a disorder or dysfunction—please make the kidneys new. Thank you for perfecting the function of my baby's kidneys in utero and for all of baby's life. Perfect baby's kidneys as they separate urea, mineral salts, toxins, and other waste products from the blood. Allow the kidneys to properly conserve water, salts, and electrolytes. Bless the regulation of baby's blood pressure and acid-base balance by the kidneys. Thank You for performing "wonders that cannot be fathomed, [and] miracles that cannot be counted" (Job 5:9, NIV). In Jesus' name. Amen.

Day 4

God, thank You for being an omnipresent God. "Where can I go from your Spirit? Where can I flee from your presence?" (Psalm 139:7, NIV) I am grateful that we do not have to wait on You to complete a task elsewhere before You see to our needs; You abide in us and are ever-present to help us. Please bless each mother who is carrying a blessing from You in her womb. Relieve the stress in these mothers' lives and help them to trust in You, LORD, with all their heart; and lean not unto their own understanding. In all their ways help them to acknowledge You, and You will direct their paths" (Proverbs 3:5–6). As my baby continues to develop in my womb, please bless my baby's growth and maturation. Thank You that baby is growing and developing at the proper pace. Anoint baby's scalp as hair begins to sprout. Please protect baby from any and all scalp problems. Thank You for being a God that attends to our every need (Philippians 4:19). In Jesus' name. Amen.

Day 5

God, thank You that You never sleep or slumber. "He will not suffer thy foot to be moved: he that keepeth thee will not slumber. Behold, he that keepeth Israel shall neither slumber nor sleep" (Psalm 121:3–4, KJV). As baby grows and develops in my womb, he or she is beginning to experience the sleep patterns of a newborn; my baby even has recognizable active and rest phases. I am thankful that although my baby may rest, you never rest. You are continuously working around a heavenly clock on baby's behalf. Please bless baby to have an accommodating activity and sleep pattern after birth. Thank You for allowing me plenty of rest, relaxation, and time to enjoy baby. "He maketh me to lie down in green pastures: He leadeth me beside the still waters" (Psalm 23:2, KJV). In Jesus' name. Amen.

Day 6

God, thank You that goodness and mercy follows me. "Surely goodness and mercy shall follow me all the days of my life" (Psalm 23:6, KJV). We are grateful that goodness and mercy are continuously following my baby and me. Baby is continuing to make exponential changes within my womb. Baby's buds for permanent teeth will soon develop. Please bless baby's milk teeth and permanent teeth as they grow in at their respective times. Thank you that baby's milk and permanent teeth are healthy and straight. Please allow baby to always maintain exceptional hygienic practices. In Jesus' name, Amen.

Day 7

God, thank You that we are heir to all of Your promises. "For no matter how many promises God has made, they are "Yes" in Christ. And so through him the "Amen" is spoken by us to the glory of God" (2 Corinthians 1:20, NIV). Many people are making predictions of baby's gender. Thanks be to God that You alone have selected the perfect baby for us—the perfect gender, the perfect size, the perfect personality, and perfect health. As baby's gender and anatomy continues to develop in utero and becomes more distinct, please bless and perfect each characteristic and each organ. Please keep and protect baby from all sexual sin and disease throughout his or her life. Help our family to stay prayerful and watchful so that we may raise our baby in the way of the Lord. "But we prayed to our God and posted a guard day and night to meet this threat" (Nehemiah 4:9, NIV). In Jesus' name. Amen.

My Letter to Baby: Date: _____

Week 20

"The righteous man leads a blameless life; blessed are his children after him" (Proverbs 20:7, NIV).

Day 1

God, thank You that we can live righteously through faith in You. "This righteousness from God comes through faith in Jesus Christ to all who believe" (Romans 3:22, NIV). We are eternally grateful for the hedge of protection you have formed around us. You have set in place a transfer of immunities from me to my baby to protect my baby from any virus that I have previously encountered. Thank You for building my immune system to overcome those viruses. As the immune cells pass from me to my baby, please allow the immune cells to strengthen baby's immune system. Additionally, by Your Holy Spirit, please bless baby's immune system to thwart off viruses I have not encountered or been exposed to. "There shall no evil befall thee, neither shall any plague come nigh thy dwelling" (Psalm 91:10, KJV). In Jesus' name. Amen.

Week 20

Day 2

God, thank You that when we belong to You, we can hear You. "He who belongs to God hears what God says" (John 8:47, NIV). Please quiet our minds and our surroundings, so that we may clearly hear You. We pray that our lives reflect our obedience to Your Word. As baby grows more capable of hearing noises from within the womb, please help me to regulate the music, words, and ambient noise that are transmitted to baby's ears. I pray that baby hears sounds of love, joy, peace, and honesty. Fill my mouth with laughter and my lips with shouts of joy (Job 8:21). In Jesus' name. Amen.

Day 3

God, thank You for Your mercies and Your lovingkindness. "Remember, O LORD, thy tender mercies and thy lovingkindnesses; for they have been ever of old" (Psalm 25:6, KJV). We are eternally grateful for the growth and development You have bestowed upon our baby. Please continue to impart Your blessing upon baby. We do not take for granted the intrinsic details for sustaining life that You have granted upon us and our baby. As baby swallows amniotic fluid daily, please bless baby's digestive system to receive proper practice for the future digestion of milk and food. Allow the amniotic fluid that baby breathes into the lungs to continue to support the proper development of the lungs. Please regulate the amount of amniotic fluid produced within me; bless the amount of amniotic fluid produced by me to aid in the proper growth and development of baby. We trust Your plan and will for baby. "In Him we were also chosen, having been predestined according to the plan of Him who works out everything in conformity with the purpose of His will" (Ephesians 1:11, NIV). In Jesus' name. Amen.

Day 4

God, thank You for being the best thing that has ever happened to me. "Who gave himself for us, that he might redeem us from all iniquity, and purify unto himself a peculiar people, zealous of good works" (Titus 2:14, KJV). We are thankful for the growth and development baby is experiencing. As baby continues to produce and accumulate meconium (a byproduct of digestion), please control the timely release of the meconium. Thank You that the meconium is stored in the proper area of baby's intestines and never enters baby's respiratory system. We praise You for being attentive to the details of baby. "I will praise You, O Lord my God, with all my heart; I will glorify your Name forever" (Psalm 86:12, NIV). In Jesus' name. Amen.

Day 5

God, thank You for surrounding us. "As the mountains surround Jerusalem, so the LORD surrounds his people both now and forevermore" (Psalm 125:2, NIV). Our baby's heart grows stronger daily. Please protect baby's heart forever. Guard baby from all heart trouble and heartache. Thank You that baby's heart pumps the proper amount of blood at the proper rate. As baby's heart grows and matures, please bless baby's heart to be free of abnormalities and defects. Surround baby's heart so the heart is healthy, but most of all, so the heart is pure, because "[b]lessed are the pure in heart: for they shall see God" (Mathew 5:8). In Jesus' name. Amen.

Day 6

God, thank You for being our strength and shield. "The LORD is my strength and my shield; my heart trusts in Him, and I am helped" (Psalm 28:7, NIV). Please continue to be baby's strength and shield as he or she grows in utero and after he or she is born. Bless and strengthen baby's legs as they grow. As baby's muscles grow and mature, bless baby's muscles to grow healthy and strong. Please bless baby's muscle tone and muscle activity. You, O Lord, are a shield around our baby, our baby's glory, and the one who lifts our baby's head (Psalm 3:3, NASB). In Jesus' name, Amen.

Day 7

God, thank You for being the center of my joy. "Then will I go unto the altar of God, unto God my exceeding joy: yea, upon the harp will I praise thee, O God my God" (Psalm 43:4, KJV). Regardless of the circumstances that arise in our lives, You, Lord, continuously fight for us (2 Chronicles 32:8). Despite my emotional state before, during, and after pregnancy, please bless baby to be joyful. We rebuke depression, sadness, fearfulness, or any other emotion that does not depict the fruit of the Spirit (Galatians 5:22). Please fill baby's life with gladness while in my womb and after birth. Thank You for allowing me, my husband, and our baby to always find relief in You—a true and living God! "He brought [us] out into a spacious place; he rescued [us] because he delighted in [us]" (Psalm 18:19, NIV). In Jesus' name. Amen.

My Letter to Baby: Date: _____

Week 21

"Train up a child in the way he should go: and when he is old, he will not depart from it." (Proverbs 22:6, KJV).

Day 1

God, thank You for being my salvation. "Behold, God is my salvation; I will trust, and not be afraid: for the LORD JEHOVAH is my strength and my song; he also is become my salvation" (Isaiah 12:2, KJV). Lord, You are blessing baby's body to experience new developments every day. Baby's white blood cells, or leukocytes, are being produced to defend baby's body against infectious disease and foreign materials. Thank you that baby's body always produces the proper amount of white blood cells. Please bless and protect the production of baby's blood cells throughout his or her life. Protect baby from problems that will lower his or her white blood cells without promptly producing more. Strengthen baby's white blood cells to properly fight all infection and disease. Please bless the white blood cell supply of all of our family. Heal all existing and oncoming infection and disease plaguing our family. "A vast crowd brought to Him people who were lame, blind, crippled, those who couldn't speak, and many others. They laid them before Jesus, and He healed them all" (Matthew 15:30, NLT). In Jesus' name. Amen.

Day 2

God, thank You for allowing us to surrender to You. "Surrender yourself to the LORD, and wait patiently for Him" (Psalm 37:7, GW). Lord, we surrender ourselves and our baby unto You, along with all our issues and concerns regarding parenting. Please guide us in every decision we make for baby and our family. As we begin to select baby gear, clothes, and furniture, please help us to make wise choices. Allow us to look beyond aesthetics to select items with the safety and wellbeing of our baby as the foremost important factor. Let Your Holy Spirit lead us to the best products for our baby. We choose You to be our guide, so please "guide me in your truth and teach me, for you are God my Savior, and my hope is in you all day long" (Psalm 25:5, NIV). In Jesus' name. Amen.

Day 3

God, thank You for choosing us to be holy and blameless in Your sight. "For he chose us in him before the creation of the world to be holy and blameless in his sight" (Ephesians 1:4, NIV). Please help us to live according to the holy and blameless character that You see in us. Help us to raise our baby to possess and exhibit a holy and blameless character. As baby's tongue completes formation, thank You that baby will use the tongue for edification and not destruction. I pray that as baby learns to speak, he or she would speak with wisdom and understanding. Your Word says, "wisdom is the principal thing; therefore get wisdom: and with all thy getting get understanding" (Proverbs 4:7, KJV). In Jesus' name. Amen.

Day 4

God, thank You for surrounding us with Your favor. "For surely, O LORD, you bless the righteous; you surround them with your favor as with a shield" (Psalm 5:12, NIV). We need Your favor daily. Both baby and I are growing and changing dramatically. Help me to adjust to the changes I am experiencing in my body. Bless baby to accumulate the proper amount of fat in the proper places of his or her body. Thank You that both baby and I are growing stronger and that baby is becoming more prepared for what will be experienced outside my womb. We believe Your Word for baby, which says, "[a]nd the child grew and became strong; he was filled with wisdom, and the grace of God was upon him" (Luke 2:40, NIV). In Jesus' name. Amen.

Day 5

God, thank You that faithful is he who calls us, who also will do it (1 Thessalonians 5:24). We are grateful that You did not specify the *it*, which confirms that what You will do for us is indefinable—the *it* is unlimited. Lord, we may never understand Your greatness, but please help us to continue to grow in You daily. As we strive each day to be better people, help us not to concentrate on physical health and fitness alone, but help us to endeavor to grow spiritually. "For physical training is of some value, but godliness has value for all things, holding promise for both the present life and the life to come" (1 Timothy 4:8, NIV). Please continue to bless baby as he or she swallows more amniotic fluid and exercises the digestive system You have beautifully formed within baby. In Jesus' name. Amen.

Day 6

God, thank You for being our light. "God is light, and in him is no darkness at all" (1 John 1:5, KJV). As baby begins to sense and see the light of the outside world, we pray that he or she will also sense and see the Light of the World, who is Jesus. Please continue to bless baby's health, strength, growth, and maturation. As baby generates new wake and sleep patterns within my womb, we pray that baby's wake and sleep patterns outside the womb are consistent and befitting to our lifestyle. Bless me to be well-rested, nourished, joyful, and confident to perform the tasks required of me—now and after the birth of our wonderful baby. "You will feel confident because there's hope, and you will look around and rest in safety" (Job 11:18, GW). In Jesus' name. Amen.

Day 7

God, thank You for protecting us and preserving our lives. "The LORD will preserve him, and keep him alive; *and* he shall be blessed upon the earth" (Psalm 41:2, KJV). I am so grateful to feel baby moving within me, and with great eagerness, I anticipate the next move baby will make. As we grow closer to the birth of baby, please guard baby and me from complications leading to preterm birth. Help my lifestyle and daily activities to please You and contribute to the health and well-being of my baby. "For the temple of God is Holy, which temple ye are" (1 Corinthians 3:17, KJV). In Jesus' name. Amen.

My Letter to Baby: Date: _____

Week 22

"Thy father and thy mother shall be glad, and she that bare thee shall rejoice" (Proverbs 23:25, KJV).

Day 1

God, thank You for enabling us to fellowship with You. "God is faithful, by whom ye were called unto the fellowship of his Son Jesus Christ our Lord" (1 Corinthians 1:9, KJV). Many amazing things are happening within me and baby. Thank You that baby is growing and maturing daily. Please continue to bless the bones within baby's ears as they harden, enabling him or her to hear me and the outside world more clearly. As baby's eyes become even more developed, please bless baby's vision to be perfect. Although the pigment of baby's eyes is yet to be known, we thank You now for selecting just the right pigment for the eyes. Baby's facial features are now developed and in position. Thank You for choosing the perfect position and structure of each feature. We praise You, because our baby is fearfully and wonderfully made (Psalm 139:14). In Jesus' name. Amen.

Day 2

God, thank You for life, breath, and all that You give to us. "He is not served by human hands, as if he needed anything, because he himself gives all men life and breath and everything else" (Acts 17:25, NIV). You have generously granted my baby life within me. Currently, baby receives oxygen via the umbilical cord, and baby's body rids itself of carbon dioxide via the umbilical cord. Please bless the umbilical cord to remain in the proper position as the umbilical cord continues to grow and perform the work assigned by You. As baby's lungs continue to grow, preparing to be baby's primary source for respiration, please perfect the lungs. Lord, You alone give and sustain baby's life. "Sustain me according to your promise, and I will live" (Psalm 119:116, NIV). In Jesus' name. Amen.

Day 3

God, thank You that it is You who has made us, and not we ourselves (Psalm 100:3). Therefore, I have peace in knowing that we are fashioned by an almighty God who will take care of us. "Thus saith the LORD that made thee, and formed thee from the womb, which will help thee; Fear not" (Isaiah 44:2, KJV). Please continue to bless baby's growth and the development of baby's senses. Perfect the development of each sense and all organs associated with baby's senses. Help baby as he or she practices the use of his or her senses in the womb. Help me to properly facilitate the development of baby's senses in and out of the womb. In Jesus' name. Amen.

Day 4

God, thank You for keeping us from being utterly consumed by situations in our lives. "Because of the LORD's great love we are not consumed, for His compassions never fail" (Lamentations 3:22, NIV). Please continue to aid baby's production of white blood cells, which will help baby fight illness and infection. Bless the growth and maturation of baby's pancreas and liver. Please allow baby's pancreas and liver to perform the tasks that You have assigned to them with perfection. Regulate baby's bilirubin levels so that jaundice (or any derivation of jaundice) is not experienced by baby. Thank You that regardless of our bodies' ability to fight illness and disease, You are our healer. "O LORD my God, I called to you for help and you healed me" (Psalm 30:2, NIV). In Jesus' name, Amen.

Day 5

God, thank You, for great is your faithfulness! (Lamentations 3:23) We are forever grateful to You for always being near. We cannot always feel You; however, You have promised never to leave us, and we trust in that promise. "The LORD will not abandon His people, because that would dishonor his great name. For it has pleased the LORD to make you his very own people" (1 Samuel 12:22, NLT). Please continue to bless baby as he or she gains strength in my womb. Increase baby's weight as You see fit. Mature and perfect baby's skin. Allow the favor of God to be upon baby now and always. In Jesus' name. Amen.

Day 6

God, thank You, for You are the best thing that has ever happened to us. "But if serving the LORD seems undesirable to you, then choose for yourselves this day whom you will serve ... But as for me and my household, we will serve the LORD" (Joshua 24:15, NIV). As we prepare for the many questions and explanations baby will seek as a toddler, throughout adolescence, and into adulthood, please prepare us for every situation. Help us to speak truthfully, and give us words to say, as You did for Moses (Exodus 4:12). Even now, as baby's brain enters a stage of rapid growth, give us things to say, eat, and do to optimize the manufacturing of baby's brain cells. Please guide us to the proper learning utensils to help develop baby's brain and learning capabilities. "To God belong wisdom and power; counsel and understanding are His" (Job 12:13, NIV). In Jesus' name. Amen.

Day 7

God, thank You for allowing us to seek You. "Seek the LORD and His strength; Seek His face continually" (Psalm 105:4, NIV). As baby continues to mature in my womb, please help us to seek You as a family. We eagerly look forward to baby's arrival; however, we need Your guidance and strength to properly prepare us. We seek direction for maintaining the love and friendship in our marriage. We seek guidance on how to introduce baby to our family, friends, and family pets. Please grant us direction on what to do, how to do it, and when to do it so that we are always in Your will for our lives. We know that Your ways and timing are impeccable, Lord, so please "teach me to do Your will, for You are my God; may Your good Spirit lead me on level ground" (Psalm 143:10). In Jesus' name. Amen.

My Letter to Baby: Date: _____

Week 23

"As arrows are in the hand of a mighty man; so are children of the youth" (Psalm 127:4, KJV).

Day 1

God, thank You for being the strength of Your people (Psalm 28:8). Please continue to be my strength throughout my pregnancy and after baby is born. Baby is constantly maturing and preparing for life beyond my womb. As our baby prepares for breathing outside of my womb, please bless the blood vessels within baby's lungs to develop properly. The surfactant, which helps baby's lungs expand after birth, is also developing. Please perfect the development of baby's surfactant, as well as the growth of the air sacs within baby's lungs. There are many details associated with baby's lungs and respiratory system; we trust that You are in control of them all. "Those who know your name will trust in you, for you, LORD, have never forsaken those who seek you" (Psalm 9:10, NIV). In Jesus' name. Amen.

Day 2

God, thank You for directing our paths. "Direct me in the path of your commands, for there I find delight" (Psalm 119:35, NIV). Please continue to lead us in the proper direction as we take care of our baby that You have so kindly placed within my womb. Thankfully, we are all fearfully and wonderfully made by You (Psalm 139:14). Regardless of the size or weight the consensus wants me to be, please utilize my body type and size to bless baby. Help me to maintain a healthy diet and lifestyle. Bless my body to supply baby with the proper amount of calcium and iron required for baby's bones to be strong and healthy—now and after birth. Help me to eat enough calories so that my baby accumulates and maintains enough fat in the proper places. In Jesus' name. Amen.

Day 3

God, thank You for knowing our end from our beginning. "I [God] make known the end from the beginning" (Isaiah 46:10, NIV). Although a mystery to me, You know when baby will be born and all circumstances surrounding baby's birth (cesarean section, natural birth, medicated birth, etc.). You have always known these details. Please prepare me; prepare my heart and mind. Thank You that baby continues to grow and mature within me until the time You have planned for him or her to be delivered. As baby's nostrils open up, please perfect baby's nose, nostrils, and all parts thereof. Bless baby's nose to properly filter and warm the air baby breathes. Thank You for perfecting the nerve cells within baby's nose. You make all things good (Genesis 1). In Jesus' name. Amen.

Day 4

God, thank You for being my rock, my fortress, and my deliverer. "The LORD is my rock, my fortress and my deliverer; my God is my rock, in whom I take refuge. He is my shield and the horn of my salvation, my stronghold" (Psalm 18:2, NIV). Please let my daily walk and relationship with You be a positive example to baby while in the womb and outside of the womb. Additionally, as the enamel that will cover baby's teeth forms, please bless the enamel to form with perfection. Thank You that baby does not experience tooth enamel erosion for any reason. Bless baby's teeth to be healthy, straight, and strong. Please give us wisdom regarding the proper diet (liquid and solid) and timing of a diet change for baby. Give us strength and knowledge of when and how to wean baby from the breast/bottle and other habit-forming delights (pacifier, thumb-sucking, etc.). In Jesus' name. Amen.

Day 5

God, thank You for liberally granting us wisdom when we ask. "If any of you lack wisdom, let him ask of God, that giveth to all men liberally, and upbraideth not; and it shall be given him" (James 1:5, KJV). Lord, my husband and I petition for wisdom on how to raise our baby and how to pray for baby as he or she grows in my womb, as well as during and after baby's birth. You have given us a significant task in raising our baby, and we want to get it right from the beginning. Help us to use the Bible as our instruction manual and Your Holy Spirit as our guide. As baby continues to grow in my womb, there are some happenings that I cannot control. Please bless baby's nerve cells to properly grow together. Guide baby's nerve cells to fully and accurately form baby's nervous system. In Jesus' name. Amen.

Day 6

God, thank You for being a Holy God! "There is none Holy as the LORD: for there is none beside Thee: neither is there any rock like our God" (1 Samuel 2:2, KJV). Help us to teach baby that You are totally sufficient for all of his or her needs, cares, and wants. As the bones located in baby's middle ear continue to harden, please bless baby to hear sounds of love, peace, and joy within our homes and places in which we reside (school, work, church, etc.). Thank You that as baby abides in my womb, the loud noises that surround us daily will not be a factor in baby's peaceful rest now or when he or she is outside of my womb. Bless baby's days to be filled with peace, love, and joy (2 Thessalonians 3:16, 1 John 4:16, Romans 15:13). In Jesus' name. Amen.

Day 7

God, thank You for helping us to do all things without complaining. "Do everything without complaining or arguing, so that you may become blameless and pure, children of God without fault" (Philippians 2:14–15, NIV). Although some days are tiring or uncomfortable, please help me to hold on to the promises in Your Word (Psalm 119:50). Help me to not allow hormones or circumstances to define who I am, but instead to allow Your Word to define who I am. "But the fruit of the Spirit is love, joy, peace, patience, kindness, goodness, faithfulness, gentleness and self-control. Against such things there is no law" (Galatians 5:23–24, NIV). Please help my husband to never feel neglected or abandoned during our pregnancy or after the birth of our baby. Help our love to grow more toward each other every day. In Jesus' name. Amen.

My Letter to Baby:

Date: _____

Week 24

"And thou shalt have joy and gladness; and many shall rejoice at his birth"
(Luke 1:14, KJV).

Day 1

God, thank You for choosing the perfect name for baby, just as You chose the perfect name for John (Zechariah and Elizabeth's son, Luke 1:13). We pray that baby's name is meaningful, respectable, and consistent with Your plan for baby's life. Through Your Word, we recognize that a name carries authority and significance (Genesis 17:5, 32:28–29; Matthew 16:17). Please bless baby's name to carry authority and significance. Help baby to live a life that yields an untarnished name. Above all, let baby recognize that Your name, Jesus, is above all names. "Therefore God exalted Him to the highest place and gave Him the name that is above every name, that at the name of Jesus every knee should bow, in heaven and on earth and under the earth" (Philippians 2:9–10, NIV). In Jesus' name. Amen.

Day 2

God, thank You for understanding our desires, even when we cannot express our request and desires in natural words. "Lord, all my desire is before Thee; and my groaning is not hid from Thee" (Psalm 38:9, KJV). As baby grows within me, please allow baby's muscles, bones, and organs to increase in mass and mature in functionality. I recognize that baby's growth will require more changes of my body. Please prepare my mind to be in tune with my bodily changes. When baby's growth and my body require me to change my daily activity or habits, help me to understand the modifications that are required of me, and please help me to change accordingly. "Show me the right path, O LORD; point out the road for me to follow" (Psalm 25:4, NLT). In Jesus' name. Amen.

Day 3

God, thank You for making us glad; we will rejoice in You! "But may all who seek you rejoice and be glad in you; may those who love Your salvation always say, 'Let God be exalted!'" (Psalm 70:4, NIV). We are excited to feel baby move and kick more each day. Help us to enjoy baby's movements and love baby, just as You have loved us. "For God so loved the world, that He gave His only begotten Son, that whosoever believeth in Him should not perish, but have everlasting life" (John 3:16, KJV). Please continue to bless baby's growth and maturity within my womb. As baby grows, bless the muscular coordination of baby's hands in utero and after birth. In Jesus' name. Amen.

Day 4

God, thank You for Your Word. "When your words came, I ate them; they were my joy and my heart's delight" (Jeremiah 15:16, NIV). Your Word is a compass for our lives. Please help us to properly guide baby according to the compass You have provided for us. We ask that You would bless baby's sweat glands as they form within baby's skin. Of the millions of sweat glands to form throughout baby's dermis, please perfect each sweat gland so that not one sweat gland is dysfunctional, but they each work in alignment with Your will. Thank You that baby's body temperature is always controlled by You. In Jesus' name. Amen.

Day 5

God, thank You that in Your presence, there is fullness of joy. "Thou wilt shew me the path of life: in Thy presence is fullness of joy; at thy right hand there are pleasures for evermore" (Psalm 16:11, KJV). Regardless of how busy our lives are, our joy and completeness are in You. Please help us to take advantage of the joy that comes with being in Your presence. Baby's lungs are continuing to mature. We pray that the branches (alveoli) of baby's respiratory tree (primarily made up of the trachea, bronchi, and bronchioles) develop with perfection. Thank You that the alveoli properly exchange oxygen and carbon dioxide in the lungs after baby's birth. Bless the alveolar cells to produce the proper amount of pulmonary surfactant, and please allow the pulmonary surfactant to work with perfection. In Jesus' name. Amen.

Day 6

God, thank You for being the giver of wisdom. "For the LORD gives wisdom, and from His mouth comes knowledge and understanding" (Proverbs 2:6, NIV). Please grant us more wisdom and knowledge as we progress closer toward baby's arrival. As baby continues to grow and mature within my womb, grant us guidance on factors that will affect baby outside the womb. Baby's taste buds are forming. Please perfect the formation and function of baby's tastes buds. Give us wisdom on what to feed baby, when to feed baby, and how much to feed baby upon his or her arrival. Prepare us physically and psychologically for the feeding choices we make. Regardless of how we feel throughout each day and night time feeding, please help us to "[b]e joyful in hope, patient in affliction, faithful in prayer" (Romans 12:12, NIV). In Jesus' name. Amen.

Day 7

God, thank You for Your perfect timing. "He has made everything beautiful in its time" (Ecclesiastes 3:11, NIV). My excitement and concern grows daily (along with my body). I wonder who the baby will look like, if the baby will sleep, and how I will cope. Thankfully, I can look to Your Word, which says, "[n]ow thanks be unto God, which always causeth us to triumph in Christ" (2 Corinthians 2:14). Help me to confidently rest in Your promises to us. Please grant me wisdom and knowledge to store Your Word in my heart (Psalm 119:11) so that when concern and questions arise, I am able to encourage myself (1 Samuel 30:6). Continue to bestow health and strength upon baby. Please bless baby as he or she grows and progresses closer to the grand birth date. In Jesus' name. Amen.

My Letter to Baby: Date: _____

Week 25

"As you do not know the path of the wind, or how the body is formed in a mother's womb, so you cannot understand the work of God, the Maker of all things" (Ecclesiastes 11:5, NIV).

Day 1

God, thank You for Your sufficient grace. "My grace is sufficient for you, for my power is made perfect in weakness" (2 Corinthians 19:2, NIV). We are grateful that no matter how weak or insufficient we feel, with You, we are strong. As baby continues to grow each day, please continue to bless the development and maturation of baby's skeletal structure and joints, as well as baby's soft tissues (ligaments, tendons, and muscles). Thank You for baby and for the joy I feel when baby moves within me. Regardless of what we read or hear that causes us to be fretful, help us to bring our cares to You daily, because You care for those who trust in You. "The LORD is good, a refuge in times of trouble. He cares for those who trust in Him" (Nahum 1:7, NIV). In Jesus' name. Amen.

Day 2

God, thank You that all things are possible with You! "Jesus looked at them and said, 'With man this is impossible, but with God all things are possible'" (Matthew 19:26, NIV). Although some days, completing the next task (or even bending to tie my shoe) is seemingly impossible, we are grateful for the strength and ability we have in You. Please continue to bless baby as the blood vessels within baby's lungs are maturing and developing. Baby's lungs grow more suitable for the outside world each day. Bless baby's lungs and entire respiratory system to be well developed and healthy upon the arrival of baby. In Jesus' name. Amen.

Day 3

God, thank You for accepting our praise. "Accept, O LORD, the willing praise of my mouth, and teach me Your laws" (Psalm 119:108, NIV). We could never properly give You praise for Your countless benefits toward us, but You choose to continuously perform wonders that cannot be fathomed and miracles that cannot be counted (Job 9:10). Please know that we are grateful. Baby's nostrils are opening up in preparation to warm air on inhalation and remove moisture on exhalation after delivery. Please bless the function and structure of baby's nose. Thank You, specifically, for the perfection of baby's nostrils and septum. In Jesus' name. Amen.

Day 4

God, thank You for watching over baby, myself, and our family. "Unless the LORD watches over the city, the watchmen stand guard in vain" (Psalm 127:1, NIV). There is no doubt that we cannot watch over ourselves, we cannot keep ourselves alive, and we cannot depend on our own abilities. We need You, unequivocally. Please continue to take care of us and our baby. As we prepare for baby's arrival, please anoint every surface (bassinet, crib, play yard, etc.) that baby will sleep on. Even before baby's sleeping arrangements have been finalized, remove all sleeping dangers. Help me and all who care for baby to properly position him or her for sleep. Please protect baby from all sleeping disorders as well as any positional sleeping hazards. Do not let any harm come nigh baby during sleep time or awake time (Psalm 91:10). In Jesus' name. Amen.

Day 5

God, thank You for sustaining our lives. "Surely God is my help; the Lord is the one who sustains me" (Psalm 54:4, NIV). As the nerves around baby's mouth and lip area become stronger and more sensitive, please perfect the function of baby's mouth and lips. Specifically, bless baby's mouth and lips to have a great affinity to my nipple or whichever feeding utensil (brand, shape, and/or size of nipple) You find suitable for baby. Allow my breast to supply more than enough milk for my baby. Additionally, please perfect the function of baby's swallowing reflexes and all brainstem functions that affect baby's swallowing reflexes. We pray against all pediatric and adult swallowing dysfunctions. Hear, O Lord, and be merciful to baby; O Lord, be our baby's helper (Psalm 30:10). In Jesus' name. Amen.

Day 6

God, thank You for the power that endorses Your Word. "God's kingdom is not just talk, it is power" (1 Corinthians 4:20, GW). Help us not to confuse Your power with that of man, because Your power is able to do that which no other power is capable of. As baby continues to grow, please bless baby's dexterity and agility—now and following baby's birth. Each day, baby is more capable of grasping objects and controlling movements. Bless the development of baby's fine and gross motor skills as he or she grows. Direct our family to properly engage in activity to mature and enhance baby's motor skills. Guide our choice of toys, games, and activities so that baby's skills are always improved, and so that baby is never harmed by the selections we make. In Jesus' name. Amen.

Day 7

God, thank You for bringing to remembrance that which we need to know. "The Holy Spirit, whom the Father will send in my name, will teach you all things and will remind you of everything I have said to you" (John 14:26, NIV). As my mind gets occupied with my "to do" list for now and after baby is born, please help me to remember everything that needs to be accomplished. Allow me to sleep and rest comfortably, without worrying, knowing that You will take care of my needs. Please supply me with the energy and strength I need to accomplish my tasks while never neglecting to nourish myself and my baby properly. Let me focus on Your Word, which says, "do not worry about tomorrow, for tomorrow will worry about itself. Each day has enough trouble of its own" (Matthew 6:34). In Jesus' name. Amen.

My Letter to Baby: Date: _____

Week 26

"I will pour out my Spirit on your offspring, and my blessing on your descendants" (Isaiah 44:3, NIV).

Day 1

God, thank You that You are a God that cares about our everyday needs; for Your Word says that when we pray, we should say, "Give us each day our daily bread" (Luke 11:3, NIV). Please continue to be attentive to our struggles each day and help us accordingly. We pray against any sickness and disease that may be a factor of pregnancy or that we are genetically predisposed to acquire. Please do not allow gestational diabetes to inhabit my body—now or ever. If I am subject to gestational diabetes or any complication thereof, I pray for protection over my body and baby (Proverbs 30:5). If I have obtained gestational diabetes or any other sickness, I pray for complete healing of my body (Psalm 30:2). In Jesus' name. Amen.

Week 26

Day 2

God, thank You for showing us Your covenant. "The secret of the LORD is with them that fear him; and he will show them his covenant" (Psalm 25:14, KJV). We are honored to experience Your covenant that puts your laws in our hearts and minds (Hebrews 8:10), forgives our sins (Hebrews 8:12), and that grants us an eternal inheritance (John 17:3). Please help us to live—and teach our baby to live—in line with Your covenant. Thank You that baby is growing and developing more each day. As baby grows, please continue to bless our baby's spine to grow stronger and more supple in order to support baby's growing body. We pray Your blessing on every joint, ring, and ligament that comprises baby's spine. In Jesus' name. Amen.

Day 3

God, thank You that we are renewed day by day. "Therefore we do not lose heart. Though outwardly we are wasting away, yet inwardly we are being renewed day by day" (2 Corinthians 4:16, NIV). As each day presents new challenges, please prepare us to conquer every challenge (Romans 8:37). Baby's lungs are becoming more developed and mature. Please perfect the production and secretion of baby's lung surfactant. Bless baby's lungs to perform with perfection while in my womb and after birth, as You have so flawlessly designed them to do. In Jesus' name. Amen.

Day 4

God, thank You for granting us the power to do Your will. "God works in you to will and to act according to his good purpose" (Philippians 2:13, NIV). In every decision we make, please guide us into Your perfect will for our lives. As baby's many organs continue to develop, please continue to bless the maturation of baby's eyes. Baby's eyes are beginning to open and blink. Perfect the operation of baby's eyes—now and after birth. Bless baby's retinas to form with perfection. Thank You that baby's retinas (and complete eye system) never suffer from any dysfunction. Although baby will see many things in the world, help baby (and our family) to be in the world but not of the world. "Do not conform any longer to the pattern of this world, but be transformed by the renewing of your mind" (Romans 12:2, NIV). In Jesus' name. Amen.

Day 5

God, thank You for not making a mistake in the promises and the Word that You have given us. "Every word of God is flawless; He is a shield to those who take refuge in Him" (Proverbs 30:5, NIV). We call on Your Word to bless baby's maternal and paternal families. May there be peace within baby's families' walls and prosperity within their homes (Psalm 122:7). Additionally, as baby's brain wave activities increase, help our family and the people who surround me on a daily basis to be positive, loving, and peaceful. We pray that baby's brain matures with perfection while in my womb and after birth. Thank You, Lord, for continuously watching over baby and taking care of him or her—now and forever. In Jesus' name. Amen.

Day 6

God, thank You that You alone can fill the voids in our lives. "He will satisfy your needs in a sun-scorched land and will strengthen your frame" (Isaiah 58:11, NIV). Baby's taste buds are continuing to mature and develop. Please continue to perfect baby's swallowing and sucking activity and motions. Since baby can taste the difference in the amniotic fluid when I eat different foods, help me to eat food that is healthy for baby and conducive to baby's growth and well-being. Help me not to eat things that cause me or baby to be sick or upset. Please help me to eat enough of the right foods at the right times. Lord, just as a hungry stomach is satisfied with food, let my hungry soul be satisfied with Your Word. "For He satisfieth the longing soul, and filleth the hungry soul with goodness" (Psalm 107:9, KJV). In Jesus' name. Amen.

Day 7

God, thank You that we do not have to be perfect on our own, but that You perfect us. "We are glad whenever we are weak but you are strong; and our prayer is for your perfection" (2 Corinthians 13:9, NIV). We look to You for strength. When our days feel long or far too short, help us to persevere. There is much to do between now and when baby comes. Please bless baby's father, me, and our family to make decisions that are conducive to Your Word and right for our baby. Ease us into the changes that will be required when baby is here so that our new lifestyle with our baby is not a total shock. Allow us to maintain our trust that You will direct us and supply all our needs according to Your will and riches in glory. "He will fulfill the desire of them that fear him: he also will hear their cry, and will save them" (Psalm 145:10, KJV). In Jesus' name. Amen.

My Letter to Baby: Date: _____

Week 27

"[W]e will tell the next generation the praiseworthy deeds of the LORD, his power, and the wonders he has done" (Psalm 78:4, NIV).

Day 1

God, thank You for making all things new. "And he that sat upon the throne said, Behold, I make all things new. And he said unto me, Write: for these words are true and faithful" (Revelation 21:5, NIV). Because You make all things new, any and all hereditary curses, illness, or afflictions end now. Thank You that our baby will not suffer for the shame, guilt, and sin of his or her parents, family, and forefathers. As baby's brain continues to rapidly grow and mature, please bless baby's brain to receive the proper nutrients and docosahexaenoic acid (DHA) required for healthy brain development. Conversation, reading, and music are important to baby's development now, so please help me share Your Word through conversation, reading, and music with our baby—now and after our baby is born. "His righteous acts will be told to those not yet born. They will hear about everything he has done" (Psalm 22:31, NLT). In Jesus' name. Amen.

Day 2

God, thank You that You remember us from a love perspective. "Remember not the sins of my youth and my rebellious ways; according to Your love remember me, for You are good, O LORD" (Psalm 25:7, NIV). As you remember us according to Your love, help us live according to Your love. Most of what baby will learn will be learned from watching us—the parents and family. Let our lives be in line with Your Word and commandments. The network of nerves in baby's ears is becoming more complete daily. As baby's response and understanding of sounds grows more consistent within my womb, let baby hear and see us living godly lives—now and after he or she is born. As baby's ears develop, let our baby hear words that please You. When our baby is born, let his or her eyes see that our words and actions are in line with Your commandments for our lives. "And this is love: that we walk in obedience to His commands" (2 John 1:6, NIV). In Jesus' name. Amen.

Day 3

God, thank You for Your presence, and thank You for guiding us daily so that You are with us wherever we go. If Your presence is not with us, please do not allow us to go (Exodus 33:15). The world offers many places and events that we have the privilege to experience; baby will have even more opportunities to experience new places and events. Guide our feet and our will to experience the places and events that are pleasing to You. Although our baby now looks similar to his or her post-birth appearance, he or she still has a lot of growing and maturing to do. Please continue to protect me from preterm labor and all problems leading to preterm labor. Bless baby to remain safe and comfortable in my womb. Help me to care for our baby to the best of my ability; for those things which are beyond my ability, help me to trust You (Psalm 62:8). In Jesus' name. Amen.

Day 4

God, thank You that through You, we are qualified for motherhood. "It is not that we think we are qualified to do anything on our own. Our qualification comes from God" (2 Corinthians 3:5, NLT). Although the tasks before me at times seem overwhelming, with You, I am more than able to conquer every task that I encounter. Please help me to first be the wife that You, O Lord, are well pleased with. Allow me to operate in Your anointing—even during everyday tasks—so that my family is blessed. Let Your love and peace resonate throughout our home daily. As our baby grows within my womb, please allow our baby to always feel tremendous love and great peace, regardless of the world's activity. Baby is beginning to practice breathing. Although baby is only breathing in water, he or she is preparing to breathe air. Please bless the function of baby's respiratory system. Perfect every part of baby's pulmonary airway. In Jesus' name. Amen.

Day 5

God, thank You for keeping me healthy—body, mind, and spirit—so that I may be an asset to my family and to those who are unhealthy. "Dear friend, I pray that you may enjoy good health and that all may go well with you, even as your soul is getting along well" (3 John 1:2, NIV). We recognize that You are a God of purpose and intent; help us to impact the lives of others according to Your assignment for our lives. Guide our rearing of our baby so that he or she is well able to live and love according to Your purpose for him or her (Psalm 33:11). As baby's eyelids open and begin to distinguish light and dark, please perfect baby's ability to distinguish light and dark—physically and spiritually. Bless every aspect of baby's physical vision. Enable baby's spiritual vision to recognize dark people, places, and things. Let baby have the insight to stay away from that which may harm him or her—body, mind, and spirit. In Jesus' name. Amen.

Day 6

God, thank You for saying "yes" to us. "For no matter how many promises God has made, they are 'Yes' in Christ. And so through him the 'Amen' is spoken by us to the glory of God" (2 Corinthians 1:20, NIV). I am not sure of how many promises I have broken to You, but today, I repent of broken promises, and I say "yes" to you, Lord. I say "yes" to Your will, way, and plans for our lives. Help us to lead baby to Your throne so that he or she, too, will say "yes" to You, Lord. Baby's retina—the nerve layer that lines the back of baby's eye—is now formed and functioning. As baby's retina senses light and creates impulses to travel through the optic nerve to the brain, please perfect the operation of baby's retina. Bless the macula of the retina to clearly see fine details. Allow baby's "spiritual macula" to clearly see the fine details of life that will allow him or her to discern truth in every situation and act in accordance to Your Word and will for him or her. "Let us discern for ourselves what is right; let us learn together what is good" (Job 34:4, NIV). In Jesus' name. Amen.

Day 7

God, thank You for never casting us away because of our transgressions. "Who is a God like You, who pardons sin and forgives the transgression of the remnant of his inheritance? You do not stay angry forever but delight to show mercy" (Micah 7:18, NIV). My love for my baby expands without bounds each day; now I have a glimpse of Your love for Your children. Baby is growing fast and has possibly grown over an inch this week alone. I imagine baby will have multiple growth spurts throughout his or her life. Please bless each part of baby's body to grow properly and according to Your divine schedule for him or her. Bless baby's mental maturation, coordination, and development to be perfected by You. As we move into the third trimester of pregnancy, give us grace to withstand any discomfort that comes with the final stretch of the wonderful journey You have blessed us to travel. In Jesus' name. Amen.

My Letter to Baby: Date: _____

Week 28

"Honour thy father and thy mother: that thy days may be long upon the land which the LORD thy God giveth thee" (Exodus 20:12, KJV).

Day 1

God, thank You that there is stability in You. "He alone is my rock and my salvation; he is my fortress, I will never be shaken" (Psalm 62:2, NIV). When there is instability all around us, we find solidity in You, Lord. Help us to continuously look to You for direction, whether there is peace or turmoil about us; please look on us with favor (Psalm 84:9). Our baby is beginning to blink. We recognize that You have created blinking to be a necessary activity to keep foreign objects out of our eyes; therefore, please bless the motion, speed, and accuracy of baby's blinking. Thank You for always keeping baby's eyes safe from foreign, sharp, or any harmful objects. In Jesus' name. Amen.

Day 2

God, thank You for never disregarding us. "Can a mother forget the baby at her breast and have no compassion on the child she has borne? Though she may forget, I will not forget you!" (Isaiah 49:15, NIV) Please anoint me to not just be a wife and mother, but instead, to be a thriving helpmeet and successful developer of Christian soldiers. Let me always find my support and strength in You. Allow me to teach our baby that You are a consistent God, never to abandon us. Studies of fetal brain wave activity show that in various stages of baby's sleep cycle, baby is dreaming. Please bless baby to have sweet dreams—now and after his or her birth. I pray that my baby is never disturbed by nightmares and unhappy dreams. Bless baby to be successful in accomplishing his or her goals and dreams according to Your will. "Then the way you live will always honor and please the Lord, and your lives will produce every kind of good fruit. All the while, you will grow as you learn to know God better and better. We also pray that you will be strengthened with all his glorious power so you will have all the endurance and patience you need. May you be filled with joy" (Colossians 1:10–11, NLT). In Jesus' name. Amen.

Day 3

God, thank You for opening our understanding to Your will. "The Sovereign LORD has given me his words of wisdom, so that I know how to comfort the weary. Morning by morning he wakens me and opens my understanding to his will" (Isaiah 50:4, NLT). We are grateful that our will is not always Your will. Please help us to more readily walk in Your will for our lives. As baby grows, help him or her to not be frustrated when his or her will is not Your will. Allow us to teach our baby that waiting on You and walking in Your will, Lord, always yields the perfect outcome. While in my womb, baby is now learning to cough, intensely suck, and breathe even better.

Though seemingly minute, these activities are significant to baby's growth. Please perfect baby's coughing, sucking, and breathing. In Jesus' name. Amen.

Day 4

God, thank You for not growing weary of my flaws. "All beautiful you are, my darling; there is no flaw in you" (Song of Solomon 4:7, NIV). I am fascinated by Your love for us, Lord. As my baby grows in my womb, I fall deeper in love with my baby daily, and I can more clearly understand Your endless love for us. There are many decisions to make regarding baby's future. How early should we teach baby to read? Should we utilize organic foods, materials, and cleaners? Will utilizing cloth or disposable diapers make a difference in baby's life? The questions are endless, but You are always near to answer every question. "Before they call I will answer; while they are still speaking I will hear" (Isaiah 65:24, NIV). Help us to bring our concerns to You. In Jesus' name. Amen.

Day 5

God, thank You for new mercies. "His mercies begin afresh each morning" (Lamentations 3:23, NLT). We know that we are undeserving of Your mercy; nevertheless, we are very appreciative that You continuously extend to us new mercies. We pray now for blended families. Whether within our immediate family, distant family, or friends, someone we know has to contend with blending one or more families. Please let Your love be a common interest between the families. Help the families to build one another up and serve one another with love (Galatians 5:13). Where a new baby is involved, allow the baby to feel a united family love. Bless the baby to never be hindered or hurt because of a divisive family. In Jesus' name. Amen.

Day 6

God, thank You for the many freedoms You have afforded to us. Please help us so that the exercise of our freedom does not become a stumbling block to the weak (1 Corinthians 8:9). Allow our family's daily actions to draw men to You, let them see You in us, and make them want to know the God we serve. As baby grows within my womb, elements within my blood become more of a factor to the health of baby. Regardless of whether my blood test has revealed that I am Rh (substance found in red blood cells of many people) positive or negative, please let the blood of Jesus be the common factor in my blood and baby's blood that prevents all sickness and disease. If I require the Rh immune globulin vaccine, allow the vaccine to be administered appropriately and in a timely manner. In Jesus' name. Amen.

Day 7

God, thank You for shining the light of your glory on our lives. "For God, who said, 'Let light shine out of darkness', made his light shine in our hearts to give us the light of the knowledge of the glory of God in the face of Christ" (2 Corinthians 4:6). Allow baby to always reflect Your shining light. As baby begins to settle into position in preparation for birth, please situate baby so he or she does not irritate my sciatic nerve. Please reduce and diminish any pain associated with the positioning of my baby within my womb. Bless baby's position to be conducive to an easy and safe delivery. In Jesus' name. Amen.

My Letter to Baby: Date: _____

Week 29

"From birth I have relied on you; you brought me forth from my mother's womb. I will ever praise you" (Psalm 71:6, NIV).

Day 1

God, thank You for protecting our minds. "And even as they did not like to retain God in their knowledge, God gave them over to a reprobate mind, to do those things which are not convenient" (Romans 1:28, KJV). We pray for those who have been given over to a reprobate mind. Steer their hearts and minds back to You. Whether these people are family members, friends, loved ones, or strangers, please return them to You. "If ye do return unto the LORD with all your hearts, then put away the strange gods … and prepare your hearts unto the LORD, and serve him only" (1 Samuel 7:3, KJV). Bless our baby to continuously retain the knowledge of You and never be given over to a reprobate mind. As baby grows in my womb more each day, continue to bless the growth and maturation of our baby. Allow the proper amount of fat to continue growing beneath baby's skin. Thank You for preparing baby's body now for properly growing and maturing outside the womb. In Jesus' name. Amen.

Day 2

God, thank You for sustaining us, because even at our best, we are nothing in comparison to Your greatness. "Because the foolishness of God is wiser than men; and the weakness of God is stronger than men" (1 Corinthians 1:25, KJV). Baby's brain is learning to control breathing as well as body temperature; however, we know that You, God, have full control. Please properly regulate baby's brain, breathing, and body temperature—now and after the birth. Thank You that baby's brain, breathing, and body temperature are perfected by You. Please be baby's sustainer when his or her thinking, breathing, or body temperature are abnormal. Now and forever, when we are weak, please be our strength (Psalm 28:8). In Jesus' name. Amen.

Day 3

God, thank You for seeing our potential to be great parents. "For I will have respect unto you, and make you fruitful, and multiply you, and establish my covenant with you" (Leviticus 26:9, KJV). As parents, help us to remember that when trouble comes or our enemy rises up against our family, one can chase a thousand, and two can put ten thousand to flight, because you are our help (Deuteronomy 32:30). While our baby continues to mature in my womb, please perfect the function of baby's eyes. Bless baby's eyes to move properly within baby's eye sockets. Thank You that each part of baby is becoming more complete daily. In Jesus' name. Amen.

Day 4

God, thank You that we are not alone in making decisions, but we can look to You. "I will lift up mine eyes unto the hills, from whence cometh my help" (Psalm 121:1, KJV). I recognize that I am only human, and alone, I make mistakes, but Your guidance will help me to discern what is best (Philippians 1:10). Please direct my footsteps so that I may not enter a place that is harmful to me or my baby. Guide my path so that my actions and reactions satisfy You and keep our baby from harm. Thank You for continuing to strengthen our baby daily within my womb. In Jesus' name. Amen.

Day 5

God, thank You for making our hearts sensitive to You and to serving Your people. "I will give you a new heart and put a new spirit in you; I will remove from you your heart of stone and give you a heart of flesh" (Ezekiel 36:26, NIV). When You changed my heart, You changed my life. Allow my life to reflect You more everyday. Help me to never revert to the person who did not know You. As baby continues to grow in my womb, he or she is becoming more sensitive to changes in light, sound, taste, and smell. This is amazing! The being inside me is able to utilize the many senses You have blessed us with. Please perfect baby's senses and abilities. Additionally, as we all grow in You, make each of our hearts sensitive to the things of God (Jeremiah 24:7). In Jesus' name. Amen.

Day 6

God, thank You for making Your way known unto us. "Teach me your way, O LORD, and I will walk in your truth; give me an undivided heart, that I may fear your name" (Psalm 86:11, NIV).

Please do not allow situations within my life to turn my heart from You. As baby grows into adulthood, help him or her to remain focused on Your Word, despite life's circumstances and situations. If not in place, baby is beginning to move into the birthing position. As my baby moves and turns within me, please keep both baby and I safe from hurt, harm, and discomfort. In Jesus' name. Amen.

Day 7

God, thank You for washing away our sins. "Arise, and be baptized, and wash away thy sins, calling on the name of the Lord" (Acts 22:16, NIV). Please don't allow our children to make the mistakes we made. Help baby to live according to Your plan for his or her life. As our baby grows closer to their birth date, please safely lead baby down the unknown paths that life will bring. Make darkness light before baby, and make the crooked ways that lay in baby's path straight (Isaiah 42:16). In Jesus' name. Amen.

My Letter to Baby: Date: _____

Week 30

*"Through him all things were made;
without him nothing was made that has been made"
(John 1:3, NIV).*

Day 1

God, thank You for allowing us to have a relationship with You. "So now we can rejoice in our wonderful new relationship with God because our Lord Jesus Christ has made us friends of God" (Romans 5:11, NLT). We are comforted in knowing that we are friends of such a mighty God. You have systematically created our baby's bone marrow to be in charge of red blood cell production. Baby's red blood cells will continuously transport oxygen and remove carbon monoxide and other gases from baby's body. Please bless baby's bone marrow to produce the proper amount of red blood cells at the proper times. Bless baby's red blood cells to accurately transport oxygen throughout baby's body and remove the proper gases from the body. I thank You that baby's bone marrow and red blood cells always work with perfection according to Your promise to perfect that which concerns us (Psalm 138:8). In Jesus' name. Amen.

Day 2

God, thank You for choosing us to be voices for You. "We are therefore Christ's ambassadors, as though God were making His appeal through us" (2 Corinthians 5:20, NIV). Help us to never be afraid to share the good news of Jesus. Baby's head is growing larger in preparation for rapid brain growth. Help us to teach baby—now and after birth—by exposing him or her to music, literature, and speech. Bless each teacher our baby will ever have, whether formally or informally. Bless the teacher's life and abilities. Anoint baby with great learning ability. Allow our baby to learn independently and in corporate settings. Above all, let Your Holy Spirit be baby's teacher. "But the Counselor, the Holy Spirit, whom the Father will send in my name, will teach you all things" (John 14:26). In Jesus' name. Amen.

Day 3

God, thank You for Your everlasting love and for the blessings in our lives. "For the LORD is good; His mercy is everlasting; and His truth endureth to all generations" (Psalm 100:5, KJV). I am comforted to know that Your truth is good for baby's generation and beyond. Bless baby to know You earlier and better than myself. My baby is growing and continuously filling my uterus. As baby fills my uterus, my amniotic fluid decreases. Please continue to properly manage the levels and performance of my amniotic fluid. Allow my amniotic fluid to continue to cushion baby, prevent umbilical cord problems, maintain the proper temperature in my womb, protect the baby against infection, and perform all other tasks you have assigned to the amniotic fluid. Please do not allow oligohydramnios (too little amniotic fluid) or hydramnios (too much amniotic fluid) to occur. In Jesus' name. Amen.

Day 4

God, thank You that this is the time of Your favor! "For he says, 'In the time of my favor I heard you, and in the day of salvation I helped you.' I tell you, now is the time of God's favor, now is the day of salvation" (2 Corinthians 6:2, NIV). If not for Your salvation, all of our efforts to live "good" lives would be in vain. Please let Your favor continue to be upon our family. Bless our baby to always be a recipient of Your favor. Baby's eyes are practicing opening, closing, and side-to-side movement. Please bless baby's eyes, eye components, and all details thereof. Thank You for perfecting baby's eyesight as his or her eyes focus after birth. In Jesus' name. Amen.

Day 5

God, thank You for the precious blood of the Lamb. "For you know that it was not with perishable things such as silver or gold that you were redeemed from the empty way of life handed down to you from your forefathers, but with the precious blood of Christ, a lamb without blemish or defect" (1 Peter 1:18–19, NIV). Carrying my precious baby helps me to better recognize the sacrifice You made in giving Your only begotten son. Thank You. Please help us to teach our baby the significance of Your sacrifice and that the sacrifice You require from us is a broken spirit and contrite heart (Psalm 51:17). As baby's body makes changes each day, please continue to bless the cycle of the lanugo (as it begins to disappear from the baby's skin) and the growth of hair on baby's head. Bless the growth, texture, and color of baby's hair. I thank You that baby never has hair dysfunction and the hair grows just as you have intended. In Jesus' name. Amen.

Day 6

God, thank You for enabling us to walk in the way of the Lord so that we may live and prosper. "Walk in all the way that the LORD your God has commanded you, so that you may live and prosper and prolong your days in the land that you will possess" (Deuteronomy 5:33, NIV). Lord, often the details of life cause us to question whether we are walking in the right direction. Help us to follow Your steps as You lead us down the right paths. Grant us wisdom to guide our baby in the way of the Lord—starting now. The details of baby's hands and feet are entering their final stages; please perfect each detail. Most of all, grant baby's hands and feet the special sense to follow You. "It is the LORD your God you must follow, and him you must revere" (Deuteronomy 13:4, NIV). In Jesus' name. Amen.

Day 7

God, thank You that You have not tested us to harm us, but to determine the faithfulness of our hearts. "You shall remember all the way which the LORD your God has led … that He might humble you, testing you, to know what was in your heart, whether you would keep His commandments or not" (Deuteronomy 8:2, NIV). Baby is now capable of producing tears, even within my womb. Prepare our family to care for baby without being stressed or overwhelmed. Although baby is sure to shed tears, please bless baby to not be colicky or cry unnecessarily. As baby grows into adulthood, please help baby to live a life that does not produce unnecessary pain and tears. In Jesus' name. Amen.

My Letter to Baby: Date: _____

Week 31

"The baby in my womb leaped for joy" (Luke 1:44, NIV).

Day 1

God, thank You for allowing us to boast about knowing You. "Let not the wise man boast of his wisdom or the strong man boast of his strength or the rich man boast of his riches, but let him who boasts boast about this: that he understands and knows me" (Jeremiah 9:23–24). Lord, often our boasting is misdirected, when You alone are great. It is You who keeps us, provides for us, and is taking care of our baby. When people credit us, help us to direct our boasting to You. As baby develops and fattens inside of my womb, please continue to take care of baby. Let our baby hear of our boast unto the Lord for the great things you have done (Psalm 44:8). In Jesus' name. Amen.

Day 2

God, thank You for guiding us in truth and right decisions; help us to not judge by what we see with our eyes or decide by what we hear with our ears (Isaiah 11:3). Daily, we make decisions that will affect our future and our baby's future. Help us to make sound decisions by listening to You and being obedient. Let us not make anxious decisions, but patiently wait for answers from You. As calcium, phosphorus, and iron are being stored within baby's bones, allowing baby's bones to grow and harden, please bless ample calcium, phosphorus, and iron to be supplied to my baby. Where I am lacking any substance that baby requires for growth, please supply all that baby needs with Your spiritual substance. Please perfect baby and my calcium, phosphorus, and iron levels. In Jesus' name. Amen.

Day 3

God, thank You for granting us dominion over so much. "And God said, Let us make man in our image, after our likeness: and let them have dominion … over all the earth" (Genesis 1:26, KJV). Please help us to handle our gift of dominion with care and teach our baby to handle this gift of dominion with care. Many times, we worry over what type of food to eat for baby's healthy brain development and proper growth, as well as what to eventually feed our baby. Please guide us in Your perfect will. Direct us to purchase, grow, cook, or make foods that are conducive to good health and long life. Although we strive to be cautious in our eating and drinking, help us not to fret (Matthew 6:25). Additionally, as baby's brain enters a new period of rapid growth and development, please bless baby to produce the hundreds of billions of healthy nerve cells that You assigned for production even before time. Regardless of my eating habits, please help baby's brain and body to be perfect according to Your predetermined will. In Jesus' name. Amen.

Day 4

God, thank You for allowing Your song of good news to be in our hearts so that we may reflect on your goodness to us. "My heart is confident in you, O God; no wonder I can sing Your praises with all my heart!" (Psalm 108:1, NLT) Regardless of my emotions or state of being, please place a song in my heart that gives You glory, Lord, because You never cease to be worthy of all praise and honor. As baby hears the music that I sing and play, bless the music to be beneficial to my baby. Let baby find joy and tranquillity in hearing music that praises You—now and outside the womb. As we fill our home and car with music that praises You, please fill our lives with peace and joy. "I will sing to the LORD, for he has been good to me" (Psalm 13:6, NIV). In Jesus' name. Amen.

Day 5

God, thank You for granting us zeal to work while we have strength. "Never be lacking in zeal, but keep your spiritual fervor, serving the Lord" (Romans 12:11, NIV). The need for rest versus the requirement to get more tasks accomplished is an ongoing battle. Please help me balance rest and the completion of tasks properly. Grant me direction so that I am not lost in the tasks of the day. As baby grows and moves more intensely in my womb, please help me to maintain a healthy lifestyle conducive to the proper growth of baby. Help me to never be disturbed by the movement of my baby in my womb, but to enjoy each movement, for the movement is a sign that baby is active and healthy. In Jesus' name. Amen.

Day 6

God, thank You for enabling us to rest. "The LORD replied, 'My Presence will go with you, and I will give you rest'" (Exodus 33:14, NIV). We have great joy in knowing that Your promises, Lord, are to every generation. Thank You that Your presence shall also go with baby and will give baby rest. As baby's lungs continue to develop, please strengthen and mature baby's respiratory system. Although we cannot continuously see what is going on within my womb, help us to continuously trust You to take care of our baby. "The LORD is good, a refuge in times of trouble. He cares for those who trust in him" (Nahum 1:7, NIV). In Jesus' name. Amen.

Day 7

God, thank You for providing all we need as we make lifestyle changes in preparation for baby's arrival. "And God is able to make all grace abound toward you; that ye, always having all sufficiency in all things, may abound to every good work" (2 Corinthians 9:8, KJV). As we make changes in our lives—whether changes of car, house, or job—help us always to make decisions that are pleasing to You. Please let the changes we make never be in regression, but always in progression as we work to be more Christ-like. (Philippians 3:10). In Jesus' name. Amen.

My Letter to Baby: Date: _____

Week 32

"Thanks be to God for His indescribable gift!"
(2 Corinthians 9:15, NKJV).

Day 1

God, thank You for daily direction. "By day the pillar of cloud did not cease to guide them on their path, nor the pillar of fire by night to shine on the way they were to take" (Nehemiah 9:19, NIV). Lord, with so many decisions to be made and an infinite list of things to do, our vision gets cloudy regarding which direction You would have us exert our efforts. Please continue to guide our paths daily. While baby discovers the newly developed senses of sight, hearing, touch, smell, and taste, please perfect baby's senses. Guide my eating, activity, and resting schedule so that baby is comfortable. Regulate my lifestyle so that baby's transition to the world is seamless for baby and me. "But You are He that took me out of the womb" (Psalm 22:9, AKJV). In Jesus' name. Amen.

Day 2

God, thank You for surrounding us with love. "Unfailing love surrounds those who trust the LORD" (Psalm 32:10, NLT). You have blessed us with a loving group of family and friends; however, when we do not feel love from our family and friends, please let Your unfailing love alone be sufficient. As the fine details of baby develop, please perfect each element of baby's maturing body. Thank You that baby continues to grow daily. Bless my baby's weight to be the proper amount—now and upon the day of delivery. In Jesus' name. Amen.

Day 3

God, thank You for the opportunity to grow closer in relationship with You. "A man of many companions may come to ruin, but there is a friend who sticks closer than a brother" (Proverbs 18:24, NIV). Earthly friends have limitations; maybe jealousy develops, or friends simply grow apart. Help us to not count solely on the friendship of mankind, but to set our hearts on our friendship with You—one who sticks closer than a brother. Lord, right now it seems impossible for me to ever forsake my baby, but if ever I grow tired of nursing, sleepless nights, and well-doing with no progress in sight, please surround baby with Your love. Let baby know that even if a woman forgets her nursing child and has no compassion for the child of her womb, you will never forget that baby (Isaiah 49:15). You are such a keeper of us that You even know the number of hairs on our heads (Matthew 10:30). As my baby continues to grow and mature in my womb, please perfect the growth of baby's hair and hair pattern, as well as the health of baby's scalp and skin—now and after birth. In Jesus' name. Amen.

Day 4

God, thank You for increasing my strength and stamina so that I am a blessing to my household and family. "Let us not be weary in well doing: for in due season we shall reap, if we faint not" (Galatians 6:9, KJV). Lord, sometimes I feel underappreciated for my contributions to our home. Please help me not to work for the glory of man, but to please You (John 7:18), because you, O Lord, will take great delight in me. You will quiet me with Your love, and You will rejoice over me with singing (Zephaniah 3:17). As baby sleeps and awakens in my womb, please bless baby to have peaceful sleep and happy dreams. As baby awakens, let baby awaken with joy to happy sounds. Bless baby to continue to have peaceful sleep and joyful awakenings after birth (Psalm 23:2). In Jesus' name. Amen.

Day 5

God, thank You for blessing us each day to nourish baby with a healthy diet. "Give us this day our daily bread" (Matthew 6:11, KJV). Without Your provisions, we would be malnourished—both physically and spiritually. Although we may not know exactly how the foods we consume are prepared or processed, You know. Please bless each step that our food encounters as the food arrives at a place of our purchase and consumption. Sanctify the food that my family and I consume, for if You sanctify the food, the food will be clean and good for us. Allow the food I consume to positively contribute to baby's healthy weight gain and body growth. Thank You that baby is healthy and well nourished. In Jesus' name. Amen.

Day 6

God, thank You for being in our lives so that our hearts are not troubled. "Let not your heart be troubled, neither let it be afraid" (John 14:27, KJV). As baby's due date draws near, I have many decisions to make. Please help me to continuously recall Your Word, which says that You do not desire for my heart to be troubled. Help me to remain relaxed, putting my trust in You. Guide me to make the proper purchases and life decisions for my family and myself. I may not have a clear view of what I want or need right now, but You know what's best for me and my baby. Please let my decisions reflect Your will (Luke 22:42). In Jesus' name. Amen.

Day 7

God, thank You for not hiding Yourself from us. "Here I am! I stand at the door and knock. If anyone hears my voice and opens the door, I will come in and eat with him, and he with me" (Revelation 3:20, NIV). Regardless of the many decisions we have to make and tasks we have to do, please help us to make time to love You, Lord. We are grateful for Your promise not to hide Yourself from us because no matter how occupied our lives become, our hearts desire more of You. We recognize that if we do not have more of You daily, then we become stagnant, which is not a part of Your will for our lives (Revelation 3:16). Help us to teach our baby to never be complacent, but to always have an earnest desire to seek You. In Jesus' name. Amen.

My Letter to Baby: Date: _____

Week 33

"For I was born a sinner—yes, from the moment my mother conceived me. But you desire honesty from the womb, teaching me wisdom even there" (Psalm 51:5–6, NLT).

Day 1

God, thank You for teaching baby wisdom, even in the womb. "You desire honesty from the womb, teaching me wisdom even there" (Psalm 51:6, NLT). Please continue to give my husband, me, and our baby wisdom (Proverbs 2:6). Help our wisdom to not fade with time, but to gain strength so that we may accomplish Your will for our lives. As our baby grows larger, more alert, and more reactive, please continue to bless the development of our baby. Continue to perfect my fluid levels—including amniotic fluid, blood, and water—so that baby is properly supported while in my womb. In Jesus' name. Amen.

Day 2

God, thank You for giving us the desires of our hearts as we delight in You (Psalm 37:4). As we draw nigh to baby's arrival, we find more to delight over—and more to fret over as well. Help us to know that the more we delight in You, the less we have to fret. Baby is getting larger by the second (so it seems). Thank You that baby's organs are properly maturing with the growth of baby's body. As baby's brain rapidly expands and matures, bless baby's head to properly expand. Please bless baby to hear the proper words and music, as well as to receive proper nutrition for healthy brain development. Perfect the hardening of baby's bones in preparation for exit from my body and entrance into the world. Thank You that baby's head and bones properly flex for an easy, uncomplicated labor and delivery (Isaiah 66:9). In Jesus' name. Amen.

Day 3

God, thank You that the pain and anguish we feel at any given moment does not compare to the greatness that will come from the suffering if we keep our trust in you. "For I reckon that the sufferings of this present time are not worthy to be compared with the glory which shall be revealed in us" (Romans 8:18, KJV). I feel beautiful and blessed to carry this child You have given me. At times, the beauty and blessedness are masked by water retention (everywhere) and discomfort; however, we are very thankful. Please continue to bless baby as the neurons and synapses develop. Baby's brain is forming connections that will be necessary throughout his or her life; please bless and perfect each connection. As my baby grows within my womb, thank You that my baby is becoming more coordinated and skillful every day. In Jesus' name. Amen.

Day 4

God, thank You for preserving us. "The LORD shall preserve thy going out and thy coming in from this time forth, and even for evermore" (Psalm 121:8, KJV). I am grateful that You personally take the time to guard our lives. When we extend ourselves too much (or are extended by others), You are careful to protect my baby and me. As baby's birth date comes closer, help me not to add undue stress to baby by over extending myself in thought or deed. Please continue to preserve us; preserve our health and strength. Baby's bones are continuing to harden; please add strength to baby's bones. Thank You that baby's bones are healthy and strong—starting now and throughout his or her adult life. In Jesus' name. Amen.

Day 5

God, thank You for teaching us to be strong and of good courage. "Be strong and of a good courage, fear not, nor be afraid of them: for the LORD thy God, he it is that doth go with thee; he will not fail thee, nor forsake thee" (Deuteronomy 31:6, KJV). Please continue to help me to be strong and of good courage as we near baby's arrival; help my husband to be supportive and encouraging as we prepare for labor and delivery. As baby takes deep breaths of water, please bless baby's muscles and lungs to continue to mature. Bless the cells within baby's lungs to produce sufficient surfactant for baby's healthy lung development. In Jesus' name. Amen.

Day 6

God, we are thankful that You enable our baby to grow. Although my husband has provided the seed to form our baby and I water (nourish) baby daily, it is You, Lord, who causes our baby to grow.

"Neither he who plants nor he who waters is anything, but only God, who makes things grow" (1 Corinthians 3:7, NIV). If baby's growth was solely up to me, I alone, could not provide all my baby needs. Please continue to bless baby's growth and maturation. As antibodies are passed from me to my baby, please allow baby to develop a healthy immune system. Help me to provide the antibodies needed for the production of baby's own strong immune system. Bless baby's immune system to protect baby from any and all disease. When baby's immune system is not enough to protect baby from sickness and disease, we are grateful that You will keep baby free from every sickness and disease (Deuteronomy 7:15). In Jesus' name. Amen.

Day 7

God, thank You for being my support. "May he send you help from the sanctuary and grant you support from Zion" (Psalm 20:2, NIV). I cannot be sure of who will be with me throughout labor, delivery, or even as I raise baby; but this I do know—You, Lord, have been and always will be my support. Please be the help and comforter that no one else can be to me. Help me to make the right decisions during labor, delivery, and as I raise baby. As I draw closer to labor and delivery, touch my mind and body, helping me to relax and be comfortable. Help me not to stress, but to trust Your guidance. I put all things in Your hands, because the works of Your hands are faithful and good (Psalm 111:7). In Jesus' name. Amen.

My Letter to Baby: Date: _____

Week 34

*"Before I was born the LORD called me;
from my birth he has made mention of my name"
(Isaiah 49:1, NIV).*

Day 1

God, thank You for forming this baby in my womb and for knowing all about my baby, because You are the maker of baby. "Thus saith the LORD, thy Redeemer, and He that formed thee from the womb, I am the LORD that maketh all things" (Isaiah 44:24, KJV). Although I cannot see inside my womb, studies show that baby now acts very similarly to a newborn. Please bless baby's movement and comfort. Thank You that baby is safe and secure within my womb. Direct my steps so that I never put my baby in harm's way (Psalm 119:133). In Jesus' name. Amen.

Day 2

God, thank You for equipping us to rejoice in our confident hope, be patient in trouble, and keep on praying (Romans 12:12). Regardless of how wonderful or disappointing our day is, You have enabled us to get through if we follow steps outlined in Your Word: rejoice, have patience, and pray. Although there are days when it seems none of these steps will relieve the matter, help us to stay focused and in tune with Your Word and directions. As baby's fat continues to accumulate, please bless baby to gain the proper amount of weight. Regulate my weight gain so that my weight is conducive to a healthy delivery of my baby and a healthy lifestyle for me after delivery. Perfect baby's growth—now and after birth. Allow baby to have a healthy appetite. Bless me to successfully supply baby with the proper amount of nutrients and milk. In Jesus' name. Amen.

Day 3

God, thank You for quenching my spiritual thirst. "But whosoever drinketh of the water that I shall give him shall never thirst; but the water that I shall give him shall be in him a well of water springing up into everlasting life" (John 4:14, KJV). Often during my pregnancy, I have thirsted for different drinks; however, I need You, Lord, to continuously quench the thirst that is unquenchable by drink—my spiritual thirst. As we continue to thirst after You, please continue to reveal Yourself to us. Additionally, bless me to supply ample milk to baby after his or her birth. Please allow my breast to overflow with the milk, nutrients, and antibodies my baby needs. Help me to properly use and store my breast milk for my baby's growth and well-being. If, for some reason, I do not breastfeed (or fall short in breastfeeding), please help me to select the perfect formula for baby. In Jesus' name. Amen.

Day 4

God, thank You for increasing my endurance. "For you have need of endurance, so that when you have done the will of God, you may receive what was promised" (Hebrews 10:36, NASB). With each step, I seem to grow more winded, and at times, discouraged; but You, God, have given me a promise. Please continue to increase my endurance so that I may receive the promise of my child. As baby grows within me, please perfect the maturation of baby's central nervous system. Thank You that baby's central nervous system never experiences disorder or disease (Psalm 91:10). In Jesus' name. Amen.

Day 5

God, thank You for being awesome. "For when you did awesome things that we did not expect, you came down, and the mountains trembled before You" (Isaiah 64:3, NIV). The mountains in our lives (e.g., fear, sickness, anxiety) must tremble at Your presence, and Your awesomeness conquers every mountain. Please continue to annihilate the mountains in our lives—those mountains that we see and those that are hidden from us (Jeremiah 51:25). In preparing for birth, baby may have already turned head-down and settled into my pelvis. If baby has not yet turned head-down, please bless baby to turn and be in the perfect position for birth. Bless baby and me to be comfortable and content as we enter the concluding weeks of baby's gestational period. In Jesus' name. Amen.

Day 6

God, thank You for establishing perseverance in me. "Consider it pure joy, my brothers, whenever you face trials of many kinds, because you know that the testing of your faith develops perseverance" (James 1:2–3, NIV). During the time that I should be most relaxed, it seems as though I have more tasks than ever to complete. Please help me where I fall short (and even where I believe I am strong). As I approach a time in which contractions (Braxton Hicks) become a reality, help me to acknowledge these discomforts as preparation for my delivery date. When possible, ease the intensity and pain of the contractions. In Jesus' name. Amen.

Day 7

God, thank You for the directives You have given us to withstand temptation. "No temptation has seized you except what is common to man. And God is faithful; he will not let you be tempted beyond what you can bear" (1 Corinthians 10:13, NIV). Each day, I face some variation of temptation; for example, temptation to fear, to worry, to eat unhealthy food, or to allow my emotions to control my temperament. Please continue to give me strength to resist temptation of any form. We pray for mommies who are experiencing early arrivals. Help the mommies to not fret, but to trust You. Regardless of when the baby comes, bless the timing to be perfect for the family and baby. Thank You that each early-arriving baby is healthy with no complications. In Jesus' name. Amen.

My Letter to Baby: Date: _____

Week 35

"They will not labor in vain, or bear children for calamity; for they are the offspring of those blessed by the LORD, and their descendants with them" (Isaiah 65:23, NASB).

Day 1

God, thank You for helping us to make the most out of every minute You have given us, now and after our baby is born. "Be very careful, then, how you live--not as unwise but as wise, making the most of every opportunity" (Ephesians 5:15–16, NIV). Please help me to rest when I need to rest; otherwise, help me not to waste the precious time You have entrusted me with. Help me recognize my limitations and wisely delegate tasks when needed. Thank You for fully establishing baby's hearing. Guide my conversation and surround me with good conversation, music, etc. so that baby is blessed by what is heard within my womb. In Jesus' name. Amen.

Day 2

God, thank You that our light affliction has no comparison to the glory that shall be revealed in our lives. "For our light affliction, which is but for a moment, worketh for us a far more exceeding and eternal weight of glory" (2 Corinthians 4:17, KJV). Often, I modestly take on the weight of burdens—mine and others. Help me to reject the weight of burdens and accept the weight of Your glory (i.e., abundance, wealth, treasure, and honor). As baby and I grow closer to the delivery day, please continue to bless baby's accumulation of fat. Allow the fat that baby (and I) accumulate to be beneficial to our bodies. Direct me to continue eating healthy food and plenty of food for the proper nourishment of baby and I. In Jesus' name. Amen.

Day 3

God, thank You for preparing us for our baby by strengthening our walk with You. "'I will strengthen them in the LORD and in His name they will walk,' declares the LORD" (Zechariah 10:12, NIV). Bringing home baby after delivery will present its own set of challenges. Please continue to strengthen me so that I grow more spiritually fit—now and after our baby is born—for no job is too complicated with You as my help (Jeremiah 32:17). Lord, as my body becomes more crowded and general movement becomes more complicated, please bless the comfort of baby and I. Help my husband to recognize when I need assistance, and help him to be generously accommodating. In Jesus' name. Amen.

Day 4

God, thank you for not hiding Your marvelous work and wonder from us. "I will proceed to do a marvelous work among this people, even a marvelous work and a wonder" (Isaiah 29:14, KJV). Often times, I feel that I have to do everything by myself, in my own strength, because that is the only way things will turn out right. Help me to trust more in Your marvelous work and Your wonder than in myself. As baby continues to mature within my womb, bless baby to continue growing to the proper delivery weight and height. If there is any abnormality in my baby or myself that the doctors have missed or that is undetectable, please heal us now (Jeremiah 17:14). We give You thanks now for protection from problems—seen and unseen—as well as known and unknown diseases. In Jesus' name. Amen.

Day 5

God, thank You for approving us to make a joyful noise unto Your name (Psalm 100:1). My heart is overwhelmed at Your goodness in our lives. Even when we cannot view Your greatness or understand Your timing, You continue to be great! Forgive us for ever doubting Your timing and Your perfect will for our lives. As baby continues to grow within my womb over the next few weeks, I pray Your blessing on baby's now fully functional kidneys, liver, and each organ. Bless baby's organs to continue functioning with perfection—now and after birth. Thank You for the blessing of feeling baby's movement within my womb (Luke 1:44–45). In Jesus' name. Amen.

Day 6

God, thank You for not bringing me this far to leave me. "Do not hide your face from me, do not turn your servant away in anger; you have been my helper. Do not reject me or forsake me, O God my Savior" (Psalm 27:9, NIV). You, Lord, have been my help, and I pray You will continue to be my help. I do not want to take a chance on hurting or disappointing You; therefore, I submit myself to You daily. I request that You renew my mind and fix my heart so that my walk with You—in front of my baby, family, and friends—is sincere and pleasing to You. Help me not to fall into the entrapment of disappointing You to please others; instead, let me please You with all of my ways (Psalm 3:6). In Jesus' name. Amen.

Day 7

God, thank You for putting time in its place. "There is a time for everything, and a season for every activity under heaven" (Ecclesiastes 3:1, NIV). Often, I allow time to control my life, but You are the creator of time, and all time is in You; therefore, my priority is not to find time to complete my daily activities, but my priority is to find my place in You. Lord, You know the exact time when baby will be born. Help me to not fret, but to trust Your timing. As labor approaches, please bless me to be in a suitable place and with competent help. Grant me serenity throughout labor and delivery, with reassurance that You are co-laboring with me (1 Corinthians 3:9). In Jesus' name. Amen.

My Letter to Baby: Date: _____

Week 36

*"God, who separated me from my mother's womb,
and called me by his grace"
(Galatians 1:15, KJV).*

Day 1

God, thank You that Your loving kindness is truly better than life! "Because thy lovingkindness is better than life, my lips shall praise thee" (Psalm 63:3, KJV). Each day, I am constantly preparing for baby's arrival, whether directly or indirectly. Please direct my preparation so that I am utilizing the time You have given me wisely. Help me to be careful about taking the advice of others without seeking confirmation from You first. Bless each mother as she approaches these final weeks (or days, for some). Please bless each baby born to not be affected by the group B streptococcus bacteria or any other harmful bacterium. If the bacterium is present at any point of labor and delivery, please let Your glorious hand hold back any repercussions the bacterium may cause. If the bacterium is known to be present and can be treated, please bless my baby and me to be treated properly. Above all, please let Your glory fill every labor and delivery room—now and always (Psalm 72:19)—so that women may feel Your precious love in a very trying hour. In Jesus' name. Amen.

Day 2

God, thank You for consolation. "When anxiety was great within me, Your consolation brought joy to my soul" (Psalm 94:19, NIV). Lord, I admit, I am not sure what life will be like when our baby joins us, and I admit that at times, I grow anxious. But when I read the word of God, I am comforted. Please bless our lives to be even more blissful when baby arrives. Prepare our hearts and home for the joy that will accompany our new life with our baby (Psalm 51:10). As baby's lungs continue to mature, please bless baby's lungs to be strong and healthy. Thank You that baby will never have a problem breathing on his or her own. In Jesus' name. Amen.

Day 3

God, thank You for being a healer. "Jesus said to him, 'I will go and heal him'" Matthew 8:7, NIV). We are grateful that Your ability to heal is not exclusive to generations past, but Your ability and desire to heal is also for current generations. As we approach labor and the delivery of our baby, please heal anything that ails me or my baby. As baby moves into the birth canal, we ask that baby moves easily and safely through the birth canal when the time is right (or safely arrives through the means of delivery selected for our baby). Bless baby to be born healthy and to continue to be healthy throughout adulthood. Help me not to fear my baby or I becoming ill, but instead, help me to take care of my baby and myself to the best of my ability. Help me trust You to be God over all sickness and disease (Exodus 23:25). In Jesus' name. Amen.

Day 4

God, thank You for helping me to exude love and patience. "Love is patient, love is kind. It does not envy, it does not boast, it is not proud" (1 Corinthians 13:4, NIV). Help me to continue following the outline of love You have given me. Regardless of the hormonal changes and discomfort I face—now or in the coming days—allow me to be conscious of my attitude toward others. Cover me in Your Holy Spirit so that I may be Christ-like in every situation (Romans 13:14)—before and after baby's birth. As the fat continues to accumulate under baby's skin, please bless baby to be born at the proper birth weight. In Jesus' name. Amen.

Day 5

God, thank You for Your Word, which challenges me to be a better person each day. "A good name is more desirable than great riches; to be esteemed is better than silver or gold" (Proverbs 22:1, NIV). Lord, You have given us free will to choose each day whether to be better, stagnant, or worse. Help my family and me to always choose to be better. Let Your Spirit and Your name always proceed our family, because if You go before us, You will make our way perfect (Psalm 18:32). Additionally, please help us to select the perfect name for baby. You have known baby's end from baby's beginning (Isaiah 46:10). Please reveal to us the name you already have for our baby. "The LORD called Me from the womb; From the body of My mother He named Me" (Isaiah 49:1, NASB). In Jesus' name. Amen.

Day 6

God, thank You for keeping us safely in Your arms. "The eternal God is your refuge, and His everlasting arms are under you. He drives out the enemy before you" (Deuteronomy 33:27, NLT). As my day to deliver baby draws nearer, my energy is more directed toward preparing a comfortable life for my baby and my family. I am grateful to know that I am in Your arms and You are taking care of the rest of life's issues. Please continue to bless baby's gums as they prepare to bud healthy teeth that baby will need before long. Allow baby's mouth cavity to always be healthy. In Jesus' name. Amen.

Day 7

God, thank You for the avenue of prayer. "If you believe, you will receive whatever you ask for in prayer" (Matthew 21:22, NIV). Help us to live so that our prayers to You are not hindered. Let us teach our baby to pray with thanksgiving and forgiveness (for ourselves and others) on his or her lips and in the heart. Baby's kidneys are now fully developed, and baby's liver has begun processing waste. Please continue to bless the operation of each of baby's organs. Regardless of hereditary diseases, always keep baby's organs safe from hurt, harm, and danger. In Jesus' name. Amen.

My Letter to Baby: Date: _____

Week 37

"I could have no greater joy than to hear that my children are following the truth" (3 John 1:4, NLT).

Day 1

God, thank You for giving us direction on how to raise our children. "Fathers, do not provoke your children to anger, but bring them up in the discipline and instruction of the Lord" (Ephesians 6:4, ESV). Although I am carrying our baby in my womb, I know that my husband is carrying our baby in his heart. Please remove any anxiety my husband feels as the delivery of our baby approaches. Help him to always follow Your Word regarding raising baby. I pray that my husband leads by example while showing love and discipline to our baby (Proverbs 13:24). While baby may be considered full term (as defined by some) and could arrive at any time, please continue to prepare baby for delivery. Allow baby's lungs to continue to mature and baby's body to grow as You have intended. Prepare my body to have uncomplicated labor and delivery. Please keep baby and me from hurt, harm, and danger during the labor and delivery process. In Jesus' name. Amen.

Day 2

God, thank You for continuously being a great God who does great things! "He is your praise; He is your God, who performed for you those great and awesome wonders you saw with your own eyes" (Deuteronomy 10:21, NIV). Lord, You have done great things for my family and me. When I have called You, You have been there. There were times when I saw results to my prayer immediately and times that I had to wait; nevertheless, You have always been right on time! As baby continues to practice breathing while in amniotic fluid, please perfect baby's breathing and all components thereof. Help me to comfortably wait on Your perfect timing for baby to be delivered. In Jesus' name. Amen.

Day 3

God, thank You for being the light of the world. "Then spake Jesus again unto them, saying, I am the light of the world: he that followeth me shall not walk in darkness, but shall have the light of life" (John 8:12, KJV). With so much darkness in the world, at times, I am afraid of bringing a new, precious life into such madness. But when I think about Your light—the light of life—I know that Your light supersedes any darkness the world has. While in my womb, baby is now able to turn toward and react to various light intensities. Please help me teach my baby how to turn toward and follow You, the light of life. Grant us wisdom and knowledge of how to instruct baby from infancy to adulthood, and help our child comprehend and follow the instruction that we, as parents, provide. Please never allow our baby to be captivated by the darkness of the world (Isaiah 5:20). In Jesus' name. Amen.

Day 4

God, thank You that we do not have to depend on man to exalt us, but that You are the God that lifts us up. "Humble yourselves in the sight of the Lord, and he will lift you up" (James 4:10, NIV). Often, we look to man for approval; however, man may not recognize all the work, strength, or energy we put into a task. But You, Lord, know all and see all—and when You exalt us, man cannot take away the honor that You give. Bless this baby to always look to You for exaltation, not man; man disappoints, but you, Lord, are loyal and true. As baby continues to grow and mature in my womb, continue to bless baby's movements and coordination. Our baby is now able to firmly grasp objects. Please always protect baby from grasping or holding on to people, places, and things that are hazardous (Psalm 101:3). In Jesus' name. Amen.

Day 5

God, thank You for giving us hearts that love and forgive. "Get rid of all bitterness, rage and anger, brawling and slander, along with every form of malice. Be kind and compassionate to one another, forgiving each other, just as in Christ God forgave you" (Ephesians 4:31–33, NIV). Forgiving someone who has been cruel is not the easiest assignment. Please help us forgive others so that You will forgive us (Matthew 6:12). As we continue to prepare for baby, help us teach baby to be strong while simultaneously having a heart that loves and forgives. Please bless baby to have a wonderful waking and sleep pattern. Help my husband and me to get plenty of rest throughout the night, even with baby's intermediate feedings and changing times. In Jesus' name. Amen.

Day 6

God, thank You for making us people of integrity. "I know, my God, that you test the heart and are pleased with integrity. All these things have I given willingly and with honest intent" (1 Chronicles 29:17, NIV). Let our family members be people of great integrity. Direct our hearts and our minds so that our daily character pleases You. Each day, baby is becoming more prepared for delivery. Please bless baby's bone and body structure, position, and weight to yield uncomplicated travel through the birth canal. Regardless of the method of delivery that is chosen or required, bless baby's structure and position to yield a healthy, uncomplicated delivery. In Jesus' name. Amen.

Day 7

God, thank You for being dependable! "The LORD is good to those who depend on Him, to those who search for Him" (Lamentations 3:25, NLT). My baby and I depend on You to be with us through labor, delivery, and life. My request for delivery is to have a natural birth without pain medication. If pain medication is required, I pray that the medication is administered to the proper place and in the correct proportions. Alone, I am incapable of completing the challenge of giving birth or rearing a child; but with You, I can do all things (Philippians 4:13). In Jesus' name. Amen.

My Prayer request for delivery:

_____

_____

My Letter to Baby: Date: _____

Week 38

"Shall I bring to the birth, and not cause to bring forth? saith the LORD" (Isaiah 66:9, KJV).

Day 1

God, thank You for being the strength of my life. "The LORD is my light and my salvation; whom shall I fear? the LORD is the strength of my life; of whom shall I be afraid?" (Psalm 27:1, KJV) As I wait on baby to come, a new fear, anxiety, or concern pesters me each day. I am glad that with You as my strength, I have nothing to fear. Please continue to perfect baby as his or her fine details near completion. Although we are anxious to see our baby, we will wait for the birth date You have selected for him or her. Please grant us endurance to wait patiently. "Patient endurance is what you need now, so that you will continue to do God's will. Then you will receive all that he has promised" (Hebrews 10:36, NLT). In Jesus' name. Amen.

Day 2

God, thank You that Your wonders are not restricted to past generations, but our children will also serve You; future generations will hear about the wonders of the Lord (Psalm 22:30). Much uncertainty surrounds this time of waiting—who the baby will look like, if I packed enough in my hospital bag, and if I am forgetting anything the baby will need. But one thing remains certain—You will continue to perfect that which concerns us (Psalm 138:8). Please continue to bless my body as it prepares for childbirth. Bless the traffic during my travel to the hospital or birthing center, prepare the nursing staff for the coming of my precious child, and prepare the doctor to perform according to Your will throughout the delivery. Our trust is in You, Lord. In Jesus' name. Amen.

Day 3

God, thank You for being our wholly God—a complete God, available for all of our needs. "And God will generously provide all you need. Then you will always have everything you need and plenty left over to share with others" (2 Corinthians 9:8, NLT). We need You to be many things to us right now—a birthing coach, a doctor, a pain reliever, etc. Thank You that You can be all these things and more. As mothers around the world enter into the course of labor and delivery, please be everything they need—at the hospital and at home. Bless each baby born to be healthy. Where complications were previously diagnosed, please reverse the problem. Replace any sickness that a mommy or baby has with perfect health. "We are glad whenever we are weak but You are strong; and our prayer is for Your perfection" (2 Corinthians 13:9, NIV). Where there have been perfectly healthy pregnancies, please continue to bless and perfect each mommy's and baby's health. In Jesus' name. Amen.

Day 4

God, thank You for Your unselfish love toward us. "This is love: not that we loved God, but that he loved us and sent his Son as an atoning sacrifice for our sins" (1 John 4:10, NIV). There is no greater love than what You have provided to us. Let my love for baby supersede my desire to spoil him or her without control. Let my love for my husband supersede the opportunity to ignore him in the busy days to come. Above all, let my love for You supersede my desire to be lackadaisical in prayer and supplication to You. The days to come may be filled with unexpected trips to the store, feedings, guests, etc. Regardless of what captures my attention throughout the days, help me to find time to commune with You and give thanks for Your unselfish love toward us. In Jesus' name. Amen.

Day 5

God, thank You for your unequivocal patience with us. "Yet for this reason I found mercy, so that in me as the foremost, Jesus Christ might demonstrate His perfect patience as an example for those who would believe in Him for eternal life" (1 Timothy 1:16, NASB). Thank You that baby continues to grow and mature in my womb. Just as you have shown us endless patience, help me to patiently attend to baby as he or she grows and matures—now and into adulthood. Grant me the patience to wait for baby's arrival. Help me to not grow tired of waiting, but instead, to trust Your perfect timing. In Jesus' name. Amen.

Day 6

God, thank You for Your gentleness toward me. "Thou hast also given me the shield of Thy salvation: and Thy gentleness hath made me great" (2 Samuel 22:36, KJV). Forgive me for taking advantage of the work Your gentleness has done in my life. Help me to show appreciation for Your gentleness by showing gentleness to others. I pray that as my days become occupied with a variety of cares, I may show gentleness to my husband and family, as You have shown gentleness to me. Please continue to bless baby as he or she grows in my womb. Bless baby and me to comfortably transition into labor and then delivery. In Jesus' name. Amen.

Day 7

God, thank You for the opportunity to possess the shield of faith. "Take up the shield of faith, with which you can extinguish all the flaming arrows of the evil one" (Ephesians 6:16, NIV). Without faith in You and Your Word, I am unable to live peaceably with myself or others. However, with faith, I am able to stand strong and believe Your promises for my life. Help me to teach my baby that without faith, it is not possible to please You, Lord (Hebrews 11:6). Allow my faith in You and Your promises to me to trump any fear that I may have for labor, delivery, or raising baby. In Jesus' name. Amen.

Week 39

"Yet you brought me out of the womb; you made me trust in you even at my mother's breast. From birth I was cast upon you; from my mother's womb you have been my God." (Psalm 22:9–10, NIV).

Day 1

God, thank You that failure is not an option when we put our hope in you. "I know that You can do all things; no plan of Yours can be thwarted" (Job 42:2, NIV). Regardless of how strong or leery I feel about labor and delivery, ultimately, my trust is in You, because with You, failure is not an option. Please continue to make my husband and me strong for the days (and nights) to come. Prepare our bodies, minds, and souls. Help us to operate as a team led by You. As my baby continues to grow within my womb, please bless baby to mature and develop as directed by You. Bless my breasts to properly prepare for nursing my baby (Psalm 22:9–10). In Jesus' name. Amen.

Day 2

God, thank You that I do not have to fear labor, delivery, child-rearing, or provision for our family, because Your Word reminds me to "[b]e strong and courageous. Do not be terrified; do not be discouraged, for the LORD your God will be with you wherever you go" (Joshua 1:9, NIV). Even better, Your Word stands true for our baby, too. Therefore, as baby travels through the birth canal (or however baby arrives), please bless baby to have comfortable, seamless travel out of me and into the world. As baby grows and travels about in life, please continue to go with baby wherever he or she goes. In Jesus' name. Amen.

Day 3

God, thank You for Your timeliness. "And a woman was there who had been subject to bleeding for twelve years, but no one could heal her. She came up behind Him [Jesus] and touched the edge of His cloak, and immediately her bleeding stopped" (Luke 8:43–44, NIV). When we act in faith according to Your will, we can trust that You are where we need You to be when we need You to be there. Help us to always be in position—both physically and spiritually—to receive whatever we are in need of from You. Please continue to bless the growth and maturation of baby—now and outside my womb. In a short time, baby will be at home with daddy and me. Continue to keep us all safe as we go and come (Deuteronomy 28:6). Let us always be attentive to Your plan and course for our family. In Jesus' name. Amen.

Day 4

God, thank You for the opportunity to intercede for others. "And seek the peace of the city [place] whither I have caused you to be carried away captives, and pray unto the LORD for it: for in the peace thereof shall ye have peace" (Jeremiah 29:7, KJV). We pray for the city and place wherein baby is born. Please allow peace and prosperity to reign in this place. Restore violence with peace, and exchange hate for love. I pray that baby is never problematic or a victim of the environment in which he or she abides; instead, I pray that our baby is always an asset to our family and our surroundings. Let grace and peace abide with baby wherever he or she shall go (Philippians 1:2). In Jesus' name. Amen.

Day 5

God, thank You for giving each of us special assignments and jobs with which to bless our family and the world. "I have seen the task which God has given the sons of men with which to occupy themselves" (Ecclesiastes 3:10, NASB). I am grateful for the assignment of motherhood that you have given me. Please direct my course and assignments as a mother. Additionally, we are grateful for the medical staff that will attend to my baby and me during labor and delivery. Bless them to perform each of their assignments with perfection. I pray for the blessing of God to be upon the lives of the medical staff members. Please help them to resolve any issues in their lives and let love and peace abide in their hearts and minds. Allow the staff to focus on the care of my baby and me during labor and delivery and throughout our postpartum stay. In Jesus' name. Amen.

Day 6

God, thank You that "the earth is the LORD's, and the fullness thereof; the world, and they that dwell therein" (Psalm 24:1, KJV). Because my baby and I are Yours, I do not have to worry; You will take care of us (Matthew 6:27) throughout the course of labor and delivery. Please prepare baby's body and the umbilical cord for an uncomplicated delivery. Allow baby to transition from within me to the world with no problems. Thank You for keeping me safe from all hurt and harm during labor and delivery. Help me to relax and trust in you. Give my husband knowledge and understanding of what to do and when to do it. Bring to remembrance Your Word and promises to us. "The Holy Spirit, whom the Father will send in my name, will teach you all things and will remind you of everything I have said to you. Peace I leave with you; my peace I give you. I do not give to you as the world gives. Do not let your hearts be troubled and do not be afraid" (John 14:26–27, NIV). In Jesus' name. Amen.

Day 7

God, thank You that the "sufferings of this present time are not worthy to be compared with the glory which shall be revealed in us" (Romans 8:18, KJV). Lord, You have created an amazing process that results in the birth of a glorious new life. We pray for the safety and security of this new life. Please bless all afterbirth processes for our baby (circumcision, shots, blood draws, etc.) to be performed safely and with perfection. Bless my physical and mental state of being after the birth of our baby; please help me to be healthy and happy. Bless my husband to be helpful and attentive to my needs and our baby's needs. In Jesus' name. Amen.

My Letter to Baby: Date: _____

Week 40

"A woman giving birth to a child has pain because her time has come; but when her baby is born she forgets the anguish because of her joy that a child is born into the world" (John 16:21, NIV).

My prayer for my new baby: Date: _____

Printed in Great Britain
by Amazon